Related Books of Interest

Audience, Relevance, and Search
Targeting Web Audiences with Relevant Content

By James Mathewson, Frank Donatone, Cynthia Fishel

ISBN-13: 978-0-13-700420-1

This guide provides real solutions to the Internet search challenges that web marketers and content professionals struggle with every day. Authored by IBM web pioneers with 45+ years of content and search optimization experience, this guide shows how to take search optimization to the next level by providing the right content to the right user at the right time. The authors provide up-to-the-minute guidance on "writing for Google" that reflects the latest changes to Google's algorithms. You'll also learn new techniques for defining keywords more effectively.

Search Engine Marketing, Inc.
Driving Search Traffic to Your Company's Website, 3/e

By Mike Moran, Bill Hunt

ISBN-13: 978-0-13-303917-7

Search Engine Marketing, Inc. introduces a holistic approach that integrates organic and paid search, and complements them both with social media. This new approach can transform the way you think about search, plan it, and profit from it. Moran and Hunt address every business, writing, and technical element of successful search engine marketing. Whatever your background, they help you fill your skills gaps and leverage the experience you already have.

D0160976

Related Books of Interest

Social Media Analytics
Techniques and Insights for Extracting Business Value Out of Social Media

By Matthew Ganis, Avinash Kohirkar
ISBN-13: 978-0-13-389256-7

Social Media Analytics is the complete insider's guide for all executives, marketing analysts, and students who want to answer mission-critical questions and maximize the business value of social media data at every step of the process. Two leaders of IBM's cutting-edge Social Media Analysis Initiative offer thorough and practical coverage of all three phases: data identification, analysis, and knowledge interpretation.

Mobile Strategy
How Your Company Can Win by Embracing Mobile Technologies

By Dirk Nicol
ISBN-13: 978-0-13-309491-6

Mobile Strategy gives IT leaders the ability to transform their business by offering all the guidance they need to navigate this complex landscape, leverage its opportunities, and protect their investments along the way. IBM's Dirk Nicol clearly explains key trends and issues across the entire mobile project lifecycle. He offers insights critical to evaluating mobile technologies, supporting BYOD, and integrating mobile, cloud, social, and big data. You'll find proven best practices based on real-world case studies from his extensive experience with IBM's enterprise customers.

Related Books of Interest

Modern Web Development with IBM WebSphere
Developing, Deploying, and Managing Mobile and Multi-Platform Apps

By Kyle Brown, Roland Barcia, Karl Bishop, Matthew Perrins
ISBN-13: 978-0-13-306703-3

This guide presents a coherent strategy for building modern mobile/web applications that are fast, responsive, interactive, reusable, maintainable, and extensible. Using well-crafted examples, the authors introduce best practices for MobileFirst development, helping you create apps that work superbly on mobile devices and add features on conventional browsers. You'll learn better ways to deliver Web 2.0 apps with HTML/JavaScript front ends, RESTful Web Services, and persistent data.

Get Bold
Using Social Media to Create a New Type of Social Business
By Sandy Carter
ISBN: 978-0-13-261831-1

SOA Governance
Achieving and Sustaining Business and IT Agility
Brown, Laird, Gee, Mitra
ISBN: 978-0-13-714746-5

Being Agile
Eleven Breakthrough Techniques to Keep You from "Waterfalling Backward"
Ekas, Will
ISBN: 978-0-13-337562-6

Getting Started with Data Science
Making Sense of Data with Analytics
Haider
ISBN: 978-0-13-399102-4

Patterns of Information Management
Chessell, Smith
ISBN: 978-0-13-315550-1

Outside-In Marketing

Outside-In Marketing
Using Big Data to Guide Your Content Marketing

James Mathewson and Mike Moran

IBM Press
Pearson plc

Boston • Columbus • Indianapolis • New York • San Francisco • Amsterdam • Cape Town
Dubai • London • Madrid • Milan • Munich • Paris • Montreal • Toronto • Delhi
Mexico City • São Paulo • Sidney • Hong Kong • Seoul • Singapore • Taipei • Tokyo

ibmpressbooks.com

IBM Press Program Managers: Steven M. Stansel, Natalie Troia

Cover design: IBM Corporation

    Executive Editor: Brett Bartow
    Acquisitions Editor: Mary Beth Ray
    Marketing Manager: Stephane Nakib
    Editorial Assistant: Vanessa Evans
    Development Editor: Box Twelve Communications
    Managing Editor: Sandra Schroeder
    Designer: Alan Clements
    Project Editors: Elaine Wiley, Lori Lyons
    Copy Editor: Kitty Wilson
    Indexer: Brad Herriman
    Compositor: Nonie Ratcliff, Bronkella Publishing LLC
    Proofreader: Debbie Williams
    Manufacturing Buyer: Dan Uhrig

    Published by Pearson plc

    Publishing as IBM Press

For information about buying this title in bulk quantities, or for special sales opportunities (which may include electronic versions; custom cover designs; and content particular to your business, training goals, marketing focus, or branding interests), please contact our corporate sales department at

    corpsales@pearsoned.com or
    (800) 382-3419.

For government sales inquiries, please contact

    governmentsales@pearsoned.com.

For questions about sales outside the U.S., please contact

    intlcs@pearsoned.com.

Library of Congress Control Number: 2016930972

ISBN-13: 978-0-13-337556-5
ISBN-10: 0-13-337556-0

Text printed in the United States on recycled paper at R.R. Donnelley in Crawfordsville, Indiana.
First printing: April 2016

To my wife, Beth, and son, John, for all their support.
—James Mathewson

To my wife, Linda, and my children, David, Madeline, Marcella, and
Dwight, with great appreciation for their support for me.
—Mike Moran

Contents at a Glance

Contents

Preface

It's possible that at this moment there are not two hotter topics in marketing than *content marketing* and *big data.* This is one of those times when what is hot is also valuable and important.

Let's start with content marketing. Perhaps the best place to begin looking at this concept is with a definition from none other than the Content Marketing Institute:

> *Content marketing is a strategic marketing approach focused on creating and distributing valuable, relevant, and consistent content to attract and retain a clearly-defined audience—and, ultimately, to drive profitable customer action.*

As content marketing is typically practiced today, however, it resembles custom publishing. Companies tell stories that romanticize their brand, distributing those stories through various channels and amplifying them through social media. Content marketing has come to be more akin to advertising than the institute's definition implies.

We have nothing against advertising, but we don't focus on that kind of content marketing. We focus on the following part of the definition: "to attract and acquire a clearly defined audience—and, ultimately, to drive profitable customer action."

The kind of content marketing we promote in this book has two distinguishing features: It is *data driven* and *inbound.* In a nutshell, our focus is on mining audience data—*big* data, if you must—and building content that will be useful in a buyer's journey. If you do it well, you turn prospects into clients and clients into brand advocates. Because this method focuses on inbound marketing—new customers discovering you—and because it relies on messages valuable to your clients—rather than about you—we call it *outside-in marketing.*

Outside-in marketing attracts prospects to your digital experiences (primarily through search) and helps them answer their questions about your products or services. If you do this in a way that respects people's time and gives them value in exchange for their attention, you can guide them through the customer journey toward purchase, adoption, and advocacy.

Outside-in marketing is extraordinarily effective at customer acquisition, sometimes bringing in four to six times the number of customers for the same cost as traditional advertising. Unlike traditional advertising, this content marketing has long-term residual benefits that can sustain a company for years with a relatively small investment. Advertising stops finding customers the moment you close your wallet, but great content can bring in new customers years after you paid for it.

Who This Book Is For

In this book, we urge you to learn your audience, focus on how you are differentiated for them, and create content that is perfect for them. We've tried to do that with this book full of content. We've tried to make this book approachable for executives while providing enough examples and practical advice for rank-and-file marketers. But this book is clearly for marketers. It's not that others can't benefit, but we don't stop to explain every marketing principle. If you're new to marketing, you might need to Google some things as you go. If you are familiar with digital marketing, you are in our sweet spot—and we'll help you get to the next level.

Traditional marketers might benefit the most, but you might also be challenged by many of the ideas in this book:

- *Outside-in marketing takes time.* Marketers are used to instant gratification. You buy an ad, you get results within a short time. Maybe the results are .01% of the total opportunity, and maybe the ROI is marginal. But the results are entirely dependent on what you did.

  To do content marketing well, you have to build for the long term. In a highly competitive marketplace, it might take months for your content to rank well in Google. And when it does, you as the marketer have little control over the results. You can't say, "I paid for those results." But you can say, "I built a team and empowered them to build the platform that got those results."

- *Outside-in marketing must be transparent.* Digital audiences are skeptical. Any attempt to deceive can lead to a brand adversary rather than a brand advocate. The best way to gain the trust of your audience is to honestly give them the information they need and let them make their own decisions. Marketers are used to hyping the good stories and ignoring problems. For today's audiences, that won't cut it.

- *Outside-in marketing is literal.* Content that works in outside-in marketing simply does its job. It's built in the plain language that prospects tend to prefer. It lacks metaphor, jargon, and "approved" company terminology. This is perhaps the most difficult concept for traditional marketers, who like to hire agencies to tell stories with rich metaphorical prose and to brand offerings with catchy names. That kind of content might work for the captive audiences of magazines or television, but it doesn't work on the web, for reasons James Mathewson explains in his book *Audience, Relevance, and Search.*

- *Outside-in marketing is in-house marketing.* Traditional marketing executives are used to taking their dollars to agencies to craft clever messages that trigger audience responses. This book is not about that. Again, we have nothing against that practice, and it might be an important part of your company's marketing plans. But outside-in methods can't merely be delegated to agencies. You must build the platform with talent that you acquire, train, and nurture. Agencies can play a part in the development of the teams and the platform, but you need to own it.

- *Outside-in marketing requires digital technology.* More and more marketers are embracing the data-driven methods we explain in this book, but they might struggle with the technical demands. Marketers must form relationships with developers, architects, analysts, and data scientists—the newest rock stars of how marketing gets done. But marketers can't just pass off the understanding of how audience data flows from one system to another. At minimum, they have to understand which data is important and how marketing strategists and practitioners best use that data to build a sustainable content platform.

- *Outside-in marketing is agile marketing.* Collecting data is worthless unless you use it to make decisions. This runs counter to the impulses of traditional marketers, who are used to reviewing and approving everything before it goes out the door. As Mike Moran explains in his book *Do It Wrong Quickly,* each experimental marketing approach might be wrong initially, but you can iteratively improve it to ultimately do it right. This not an easy sell to traditional marketers, who tend to be perfectionists.

Because this method is so radical, this book also focuses on how to transform organizational culture and systems to do outside-in marketing well. The biggest culture shift is explicit in the title: outside-in. Organizations that want to do content marketing must start by listening to their clients and prospects and building content on (and in) their terms. It's not about pushing messages on unwilling audiences; it's about pulling willing audiences to your messages. It's not about interrupting the audience with messages they don't need; it's about intercepting their search for the information they need.

What's In This Book

In Chapter 1, we further introduce the concept of outside-in marketing, and in Chapter 2 we tie the concept to content marketing. Chapter 3 is our first foray into culture transformation, where the real work of content marketing begins.

We turn to infrastructure transformation in Chapter 4, explaining how content can be targeted to its audience. Chapter 5 goes deeper into big data, as we align our content to specific steps in the buyer's journey. In Chapter 6, we tackle the role of user experience in driving customers to purchases.

The overall message of this book is that your customers have information needs—and it is in your best interest to discover those needs. If you use the data available to you to identify the needs that your offerings are best suited to satisfy, you'll be able to create content that attracts the right customers to you.

Don't settle for average marketing. Don't put more me-too content out there. Don't bore your customers. Instead, use the data all around you to find your voice—the unique voice that the right customers are waiting to hear. That's the promise of outside-in marketing.

Acknowledgments

First and foremost, I would like to thank my family, especially my wife, Beth Mathewson, and my son, John Mathewson, who endured countless hours of my absence from family events for the sake of this book. Your love and support have been essential to finishing it.

I also want to thank my co-author Mike Moran, who helped in too many ways to count. Most of all, Mike's steady hand and calm leadership helped guide the whole creative process in a fruitful way.

I want to thank my management chain at IBM®, especially Jon Iwata, John Gallagher, Kevin Eagan, Robert Schwartz, and Rudy Chang. Creativity can't be scheduled. Rudy in particular has given me the space to let it flow when needed.

I want to thank the management chain that approved this book originally, especially Ethan McCarty, Noah Syken, Ann Rubin, and Ben Edwards.

I want to thank my IBM colleagues (past and present), who are too numerous to list. But these are some of the folks who have lent clarity to this work, in no particular order: Christine Smith, Mayo Takeuchi, Lu Ai, Pernilla Lagerkron, Klim Kaval, Christophe Jammet, Marisela Riveros, Scott Farnsworth, Penny Graham, Reena Jana, Gaby Grenchus, Heather McMahon, Danielle DeGrazia, Anita Liang, Dan Segal, Damien Bianchi, Raul Navarro, Pam Gray, Chris Schweppe, Paul Henry, Jeremy Sanchez, Tom Pritchard, Meg Thompson, Denise Beckmann, Garett Hall, Jeff Ramminger, Augustine Fou, Mike Iantosca, Andrew Bredencamp, and Michael Priestley.

I want to thank the vast network of my influencers, who are also too numerous to list, but here is an abridged list in no particular order: Rand Fishkin, Danny Sullivan, Barry Schwartz, Gerry McGovern, Karen McGrane, Kristina Halvorson, Rahel Bailie, Collen Jones, Ann Handley, Scott Abel, Jered Spool, Steve Krug, and Bill Hunt.

Finally, I want to thank the authors who have inspired the linguistics, media studies, and philosophy that underpin most of my thinking, especially Dan Sperber, Dierdre Wilson, Paul Saenger, Marshall McLuhan, Walter Ong, Ludwig Wittgenstein, St. Thomas Aquinas, and Aristotle.

—James Mathewson

I can't begin my list of thank-yous with anyone but my co-author, James Mathewson. James conceived the original idea of this book and did the lion's share of the writing. Every idea in this book bears his stamp in some way, and most of the ideas are things he tried out and perfected at IBM. This book would not exist without James, and I need to publicly thank him for that.

I would also like to thank Rob Key, who has given me numerous opportunities to help clients of both Converseon and Revealed Context, and who also contributed a great interview in Chapter 4. In fact, this is a great time to thank all of the folks we interviewed: Ben Edwards of PayPal; speakers, authors, and consultants Mark Schaefer and Bill Hunt; Kristina Halvorson of Brain Traffic and Confab Events; and Jared Spool of User Interface Engineering. Those interviews bring outside perspectives to these topics, which James and I really appreciate.

The team at IBM Press, especially our editors Bernard Goodwin and Mary Beth Ray, was very helpful, especially as we took longer to deliver this book than we expected. Thanks for waiting.

I also want to thank my sister, Eileen Cosenza, who does everything at Mike Moran Group that I don't want to do, so that I can write books without going broke. I'd also like to thank Angela Wu, whose diagrams look a lot better than anything I could have done.

Most of all, I want to thank my wife, Linda, and my children, David, Madeline, Marcella, and Dwight, who provided the motivation for me to write this book as well as for everything else I do. I love them very much.

—Mike Moran

About the Authors

James Mathewson has 20 years of experience in writing, editing, and publishing effective web content. As the distinguished technical marketer for search at IBM, he currently leads four missions within IBM Marketing: search marketing, content strategy, video marketing optimization, and marketing taxonomy innovation. These related missions come together in the tools and education he designs to scale content marketing across the largest B2B enterprise in the world.

James is also a prolific author. As lead author of *Audience, Relevance, and Search: Targeting Web Audiences with Relevant Content* (IBM Press, 2010) (with co-authors Frank Donatone and Cynthia Fishel), he helped pioneer a new way of thinking about search marketing. Rather than seeing search as an after-the-fact optimization tactic, the book encourages authors to see search as a source of audience data. Using this data, authors can better understand the needs of their target audiences in their planning and writing activities. The book predated algorithm changes at Google, which force SEOs to follow many of its guidelines—in particular, write for humans, not search engines, but when you write, use search query data to better understand the humans you write for. James is also author of more than 1,500 articles and blog posts, mostly on the intersection of technology and content.

James has led the organic search marketing mission for IBM for five years, adding the other missions as the needs have arisen. As search marketing leader, James has built the systems, processes, and technologies necessary to govern content creation and curation across millions of web experiences worldwide. As such, he has been at the tip of the transformation spear, as the company has shifted from a traditional brand and comms marketing model led by advertising toward a content marketing model that focuses on intercepting clients and prospects in their content discovery activities. The transformation has contributed to a fourfold increase in leads attributed to digital marketing.

Prior to leading the search mission, James was editor in chief of ibm.com for four years. In that role, he focused on improving customer satisfaction with ibm.com content. That entailed writing style guides and educating writers, editors, and content strategists on how to create audience-centric content. These efforts helped reduce the percentage of users citing content quality as the cause of their dissatisfaction from 6% to 1%. During his tenure, search continued to cause 7% of the respondents to fail to achieve their goals, and so he has focused on search ever since. His first job in that capacity was to replace the ibm.com internal search function. Within a month, the new system went from the 20th largest to the 2nd largest referring source for IBM marketing experiences.

Prior to coming to IBM, James was editor in chief of *ComputerUser* magazine and ComputerUser.com from 1997 to 2003. Targeting techies and developers, the magazine was a monthly tabloid-style publication distributed in 35 markets in the United States. Under his leadership, the publication grew from distribution of 600,000 to 2 million per month. The related daily website grew from its inception in 1999 to 1.7 million unique visits per month.

James holds two master's degrees from the University of Minnesota, an M.A. in philosophy of language and linguistics and an M.S. in the rhetoric of scientific and technical communication. James lives in Beacon, New York, with his wife, Beth, son, John, and dog, Lily. Though he works at Astor Place in New York City, he was attracted to the Hudson Valley for its many majestic hikes and other outdoor activities.

Mike Moran has worked on the web since its inception, in both marketing and technical roles, including eight years at ibm.com, IBM's customer-facing website. In 2008, Mike retired from IBM to pursue speaking, writing, and consulting at Mike Moran Group, and he also serves as a senior strategist for both the social media consultancy Converseon and its spin-off social analytics company, Revealed Context. Mike is also a senior strategist at SoloSegment, a content marketing company specializing in website search and personalization for B2B clients. He's twice been named one of the top 50 Internet marketers and regularly consults for Fortune 500 companies around the world.

Mike is the co-author (along with Bill Hunt) of *Search Engine Marketing, Inc.: Driving Traffic to Your Website*, now in its third edition, and the author of *Do It Wrong Quickly: How the Web Changes the Old Marketing*

Rules, perhaps the first book on agile marketing. He writes regular columns on digital marketing for WebProNews and Search Engine Guide and is the founder and senior author at Biznology (biznology.com).

Mike is a Senior Fellow of the Society for New Communications Research and an Open Group Distinguished IT Specialist. Mike is a frequent keynote speaker on digital marketing at events around the world, serves as a Visiting Lecturer to the University of Virginia's Darden School of Business, works as an instructor at Rutgers University, and holds an Advanced Certificate in Market Management Practice from the Royal UK Charter Institute of Marketing.

Mike also has a broad technical background, with over 30 years of experience in search technology, working at IBM Research, Lotus®, and other IBM software units. He led the product team that developed the first commercial linguistic search engine in 1989 and has been granted 11 patents in search and retrieval technology. He led the integration of ibm.com's site search technologies as well as projects in content management, personalization, and web metrics. Mike led the adoption of search marketing at ibm.com back in 2001 and pioneered product search facilities that dramatically raised conversion rates. Mike was named an IBM Distinguished Engineer in 2005.

Mike can be reached through his website, mikemoran.com.

1

Understanding Outside-In Marketing

This client meeting was not going to be run-of-the-mill.

You see, this client was one of the largest banks in the world, with a traditional approach to marketing honed over many years of using ads on top of offers that weren't too far away from free toasters when you open your Christmas Club account. Nowadays, no banks offer Christmas Club accounts, and they don't give away toasters, but their approach to marketing is very much the same. All banks seem to run the same two kinds of ads all the time.

The first kind is very practical: "FREE CHECKING!" (For some reason, capitalizing the words makes the offer better.) We've all seen these kinds of ads, whether they are hawking refinancing with no closing costs or some other money-saving idea. They all sound the same after a while, and you'd be hard-pressed to remember one bank over another based on their offers.

Then there's the second kind of ad. You've seen them. Friendly tellers smiling as they take your deposit. The bank manager reaching out to shake the hand of the nervous loan applicant. "We're the [insert one: family, neighborhood, friendly, local] bank." (This slogan needs to be in mixed case because small letters are warmer.) Once again, every bank is friendlier than your Aunt Minnie, but you can't tell any of them apart.

Anyway, all the important people were at this presentation—the bank's Chief Marketing Officer along with a dozen minions—and they were waiting for this brand-new idea—our new campaign for their FREE CHECKING account. (Sorry about the caps; force of habit.) What they were expecting was a brand-new idea for doing the same old thing, but that wasn't what they were going to get.

The presentation began strangely, the bankers thought, because the first few slides talked about how customers spoke about the bank and about each of the bank's competitors. The slides showed data summarizing *when* customers talked about the bank in social media and what they said. This was puzzling to the bankers because what they wanted to see was how we were going to persuade more customers to choose their bank for their checking accounts. It was unclear to the bankers why they should care about exactly *when* customers talked about checking accounts in social media.

But it all came into focus when the presentation started to show data about exactly what kind of information was most persuasive to customers who were considering switching their checking accounts to a new bank. The most compelling information included reviews and other experiences related by other customers about how they were being treated by their bank.

More than any other kind of information, the data showed that the best predictor of whether a customer would switch to a particular bank was how many positive experiences they read about from *that* bank's existing customers. So the data suggested that the bank find an answer to the question "What is the most effective marketing strategy to get people to switch their checking accounts to our bank?" The data reveals the answer: Get happy existing customers to post their experiences.

As the presentation was about to turn to the wondrous array of ideas that would persuade customers to share their experiences, the CMO interrupted with his assessment of the presentation: "Okay, so we need to get happy customers to post their experiences. But how is that marketing? That's customer service!"

And so it is. In part. But it is also reinforcing through marketing that customers have made the right choice. It involves explaining the additional services that let customers bank online, such as text messages when their balance gets too low, crediting their paycheck deposits immediately, and five other things that they might not know about. There were dozens of ideas in that presentation about how the right kind of marketing content, delivered to the right customer, at the right time, could persuade them to share their experiences.

Those ideas weren't ads. They were content marketing campaigns. They were emails that explained how to avoid identity theft. They were microsites that help balance a checkbook. They were videos that explained how to tie your checking account to Quicken. They weren't ads. They were crafted pieces of content that were helpful to customers. In many ways, these ideas weren't very different from the blizzards of pamphlets every bank surrounds its tellers with—but in this case, the content was being found before anyone went to the bank.

The CMO wasn't entirely convinced at first, but he was open-minded enough to give it a try. Most of the ideas didn't work, but a few of them did. We knew which ones worked because we measured the results. You see, we had a lot of good ideas, but we had a lot of bad ones, too. We didn't really know which content ideas were the good ones until we let the data tell us.

And that's what this book is about.

It's about a different kind of marketing—content marketing. People can define content marketing in many ways, but it is certainly not your father's advertising. Content marketing is informative, entertaining, and helpful. But great ideas for content aren't enough. Who decides they are "great"? The customer decides. How do we know the decision of the customer? Data— the more the better.

Content marketing and big data go together like FREE and CHECKING. Content marketing provides value to the customer even if the product is never purchased. Big data provides the feedback loop that determines which content is really working.

We call this *outside-in* marketing because it begins with listening to clients and prospects and understanding what language resonates with them. It then uses this data (okay, *big* data) to help craft compelling, useful content for those audiences. Only after the content is published do you know if it really worked. But it will never work if you don't listen for the needs of your clients and prospects and then develop what they need.

It rarely works to push inside-out FREE CHECKING!–style messages on an audience. We have found through hundreds of client engagements that outside-in marketing is just more effective. This book will show you how to transform your marketing organization from an inside-out model to an outside-in model.

What Is Outside-In Marketing?

Outside-in marketing is the practice of learning the language of your clients and prospects and building messages for them on (and in) their terms. This might seem like an obvious thing to do, but until recently, it was rarely practiced in industry. Typically, marketers have sought to differentiate their products by branding them with clever names and marketing them with novel messages. Let's call this inside-out marketing, to distinguish it from what we are attempting to promote in this book.

If you've ever suffered through a radio commercial at three times the normal volume for a local car dealership where the announcer races through three minutes of script in 30 seconds, you've experienced inside-out marketing. One of the biggest goals of inside-out marketing is to get attention—to get the audience to wake from its reverie to actually listen, watch, or read the message in front of them.

Inside-out marketing worked in the days of captive audiences, who passively watched TV or read periodicals. Perhaps it worked when events were the center of marketing campaigns and those who attended events were captivated by pomp and circumstance. But inside-out marketing does not work in digital media. Digital audiences are not captive. They are in control. They reject attempts to spam them with information they don't want. Any attempt to do this can do more harm than good.

If you want to be effective in digital marketing, you need to engage with clients and prospects on their terms. You need to build trust with them by providing the information they need when they need it. And you need to continuously prove to them that you will not violate this trust by trying to force them to do business on *your* terms.

The good news is that clients and prospects actually tell you what they *want* by searching for things in Google, Bing, and other search engines. Throughout this book, we refer to anything the searcher types into the search box as a *keyword*. The second piece of good news is that they tell you what they *think* about what they want in social media. All you need to do is gather the data and mine it to better address what clients and prospects need from your marketing activities.

Gathering the data might be the easy part. Everybody has access to search keyword tools, such as Google Keyword Planner. Most of us can find more conversations through social listening tools, such as Salesforce's Social Studio (formerly Radian6). The challenge lies in analyzing the data we find. When customers enter a keyword, what exactly are they looking for? We assume that they're looking for something related to the topic expressed by the keyword. But exactly what do they want? And what do they need to do with the information once they get it?

It is not helpful to merely offer encyclopedic amounts of information. You must help prospects take action to actually solve their problem with the information you help them find. But what actions do they want to take? How can you learn this from a few simple search keywords and some social conversations?

You are not serving your client if you merely mine the data. Clients expect you to recommend the right things for them to do. They want to be told what to do, in words of two syllables or less. They might be experts in what they do, but they are not experts in what you do—until you make them so.

We will start to answer these questions in this chapter and continue throughout the book. To answer these questions, we want to more strongly differentiate outside-in from inside-out marketing. Table 1-1 shows the differences. As we refine the definition of outside-in marketing, we can begin to answer how to do it.

Table 1-1   The Major Differences Between Inside-Out and Outside-In Marketing

Inside-Out Marketing	Outside-In Marketing
Uses company terminology	Uses audience language
Pushes content chosen by the company to the audience	Pulls content chosen by the audience from the company
Requires heavy and broad advertising	Requires narrow advertising, if any
Interrupts audiences with the message the company wants to send	Intercepts audiences with content that meets their needs
Has a short shelf life and consists of many one-time campaigns	Has the long shelf life of a perpetual campaign
Uses fragmented media approaches	Uses an integrated media approach
Uses a waterfall development approach, where work is thoroughly planned up front and executed without change until the entire project is finished	Uses an agile development approach, where you start small, with ideas tested and modified throughout the execution of the project, based on what's working and what's not
Employs search and social media as an after-the-fact tactic	Integrates digital, search, and social media throughout the entire campaign
Clutters the user experience with many messages	Creates a unified user experience with an integrated message

Is Outside-In Marketing Really That Different?

The ideas discussed so far in this chapter seem like Marketing 101—all the same things we have always done with offline media. And, indeed, there are similarities. Direct marketers, for example, have long used customer insights and optimization metrics to improve results over time. Copywriters have for many years built audience personas and written audience-centric copy. And advertisers have always tried to place ads at the decision point for their audience.

Direct Marketing: Push vs. Pull

When you consider the psychology of direct marketing, you realize that it is fundamentally different from outside-in marketing. Leaving junk mail and other spammy methods aside, the best direct marketers use facts about the target audience to try to understand what they need and push it to them. In that respect, it is outside-in, right? Well, not exactly.

For example, James recently moved and had to notify the U.S. Postal Service of his change of address. When he opened the envelope from the Postal Service, it was full of ads for home improvement centers, insurance firms, and other businesses commonly frequented by those who have recently moved. After he moved, he received the same ads in direct mail that had been included in the envelope. Not only did those companies know he probably would need to do business with companies like the ones in the ads, but they knew how to reach him most effectively, by repeating the ads multiple times. In psychology, this is called *priming*—repeating the same message multiple times to get a desired result. Direct marketers have used this technique successfully for decades.

The key difference between outside-in and (well-done) direct marketing is in the word *push* you probably noticed. Direct marketers push messages to those who are somewhat likely to be interested in them. They don't wait for the audience to tell them that they are in fact interested. They are willing to concede that they might get only 1% response for their direct mail campaigns. But, even if they do, they will get a solid return on investment. So they push messages and hope for the best. In the process, they effectively spam the other 99% of their audience. And they don't care.

The reason they get the ROI is that you are an audience that is somewhat captive to their messages. You can't choose not to receive your mail. When you open your mail box, there might be a check or an important letter or card. There will also be the direct mail pieces. You can choose to recycle them instantly, but you must at least look at them. In short, you must "opt out" of them. A small percentage of users don't opt out. These are the ones who give direct marketers their ROI.

Digital marketers have tried the push model from the beginning. But it never worked very well. Why not? Because web users are not a captive audience. They "opt in" to only the information they want to consume. You could say that opting out, such as deleting an email or abandoning a web page, is a lot like recycling a piece of direct mail. The difference is that you can keep sending direct mail to the same customer even after he has recycled 100 pieces, hoping to hit the mark with some of them, but web users are always moving and seeking information rather than waiting motionless for information to find them. It's always been called "surfing" for a reason. Automated spam filters constantly evolve for a reason.

Other techniques can cross the line from "welcome" to "spam," also. Readers believe that they have developed *banner blindness* and do not even see display ads. But marketers now *retarget* ads by showing display ads informed by searches and other activity. And people do seem to notice them, whether they click on them or complain about them. Whether these ads are "welcome" or "spam" depends on how relevant they are to the reader, but they are at least more relevant than random display ads.

Once a digital marketer violates the trust of the audience, which is based on allowing them to opt in rather than forcing them to opt out, they never come back. Over time, relying solely on push marketing in the digital world is a losing proposition, as your user base slowly dries up. Websites become ghost towns. Email newsletters end up in spam folders. And social platforms die.

While all this might seem obvious to some people, others might reasonably object, saying, "One man's pushing is another's sharing. If the content is good, why can't you push it?" And that is the real question here. What kind of sharing violates the trust of the audience, and what kind increases it? Every marketer must make the decision between spamming and sharing and must realize that spamming does have real consequences.

It's not that push marketing *never* works. And we aren't trying to get you to stop *all* push marketing. We are trying to persuade you that employing *solely* push techniques causes you to send more and more emails, to buy more and more display ads, and to blanket your audience with more and more interruptions. If 99% of them are not interested, eventually your audience will find ways to tune it all out. That said, it is also true that you need to prime your audience to help them discover you. If your content is high quality, sharing it will be welcome—and that's what you are aiming for.

If you learn what your audience needs and *pull* them into your experiences through search and social media, you will develop a loyal audience—and ultimately get better results. Users who are allowed to "opt in" to messages are prequalified as interested parties. They will spend some of their precious time and attention exploring your site to get answers. Once you gain their trust, you can begin to subtly influence them to try (and ultimately to buy) your products and services. We usually refer to this content-first approach as *content marketing*.

Unlike push techniques that must start by *getting* attention from your audience, pull techniques require *paying* attention to your audience. Because you can't pay attention to every single audience member, you analyze data as a way to know them. That's the essence of outside-in marketing—using data to focus your content marketing.

Advertising: Broad Spend vs. Narrow Spend

Advertising is designed to generate interest in a product by producing clever and visually stunning ads and then flooding the market with them. We are all so familiar with this method from iconic brands such as Coke and Apple that it hardly requires analysis. It is no exaggeration to say that most big brands were built using this method on TV and in print. And the practice is effective to this day.

The same advertising agencies that create and manage these offline campaigns tried to follow the same playbook in the digital world. Read any story in *Advertising Age* about these campaigns, and you'll find that it hasn't worked nearly as well online as it worked offline. A big reason is one we've mentioned already: Digital users are in control and choose to ignore or subvert digital advertising in large percentages. Traditional advertising requires a captive audience.

Jared Spool, an expert in user experience, simplified the argument of advertising vs. content in a 2013 speech (Confab, Minneapolis, 2013). "Ads don't work," he said. "You get a tiny fraction of the clicks on a page to ads. With the advent of smaller screens in mobile devices, almost half of the tiny fraction of clicks you get are mistake clicks—those where a user is trying to click a content link and accidentally clicks an ad."

In his talk, Spool cited case study after case study showing that the user experience of banner ads in particular is antithetical to usage of the web. Web users are typically trying to get the information they need in the shortest possible time. In this context, banner ads are just in the way, unless they are legitimately calling attention to quality content that people will share themselves once they discover it. If most display ads shared quality content, the use of ad blockers would not be on the rise.

In some cases, the only way to get users to click banner ads is to deceive them into thinking they're clicking something else. This is a sure way of destroying any trust you might have gained from them. Again, once you destroy user trust, you will rarely get it back.

Not all online advertising is ineffective. Google introduced the pay-per-click model of search advertising in 2000, and this model is the primary reason the company has a $1 trillion market cap. But this kind of advertising is fundamentally different from banners. Users who see search ads have already indicated interest in the topic by entering a search keyword. This kind of advertising works because it fits the general pattern of outside-in marketing.

Still, not all paid search advertising works. Some advertisers have tried to use the same shotgun approach to paid search that they have used in offline advertising, buying hundreds of somewhat relevant keywords pointed to the same landing page, in the hopes of casting a wider net for prospects. Because they are paying by the click, they figure they will get their money's worth.

But, as we will explain later in the book, this rarely works. The best practice is to buy only the words that are most tightly targeted to a campaign and then to pay careful attention to the experiences users land on when they click the ads. This narrow approach yields better results. We call this *narrow-band* paid search advertising.

Contextual advertising works much the same as narrow-band paid search advertising. Advertisers buy words that are relevant to their campaigns and specify on which sites they want their ads to appear. Not only are the semantics of the words narrowly relevant to the interests of the audience, but the sites narrow it further. And because you pay only by the click, narrowing the context will lighten your spend and reduce your cost per response.

And because the context is narrow, the spending can be light. You can turn your ad campaigns into surgical strikes, testing multiple variations of ads and landing pages and ultimately using the most effective ones. In short, search advertising has much in common with other forms of outside-in marketing: You use big data (search keywords or words in context) to attract an audience that is likely to buy into your offers. And you optimize the campaign over time to produce a higher yield.

Telemarketing: Interruption Marketing vs. Interception Marketing

Outside-in marketing is based on the simple premise that successful digital marketing allows the audience to tell you what they need so you can provide it. "What if your audience doesn't know that it wants what you are trying to sell? How can you attract them?" We have often been asked these questions by folks who have a vested interest in the status quo of inside-out marketing. For them, a part of every campaign involves some cold calling of prospects in a list they bought somewhere. The only intelligence they use in this method is to verify that the prospects have some likelihood to buy the product or service in the future. But they typically have no idea where the prospects are in the sales cycle—how ready they are to receive the message.

You might think that in the age of do-not-call lists and other consumer protections that telemarketing is dying. Not so. The Bureau of Labor Statistics claims that there were a quarter of a million telemarketers engaged full time in the United States in 2012. This is about the same as it was in the previous reporting period. So telemarketing is still widespread and does not seem to be decreasing, especially when you consider that robo-calls are allowing the same number of telemarketers to make even more calls per person. But telemarketing techniques usually fail or at least produce ill will that costs you in other ways.

Why? Because prospects don't like getting interrupted. Even those who tolerate interruption are less apt to act favorably to these interruptions for a simple reason: It takes a lot of mental effort to change one's train of thought. Think about the last time you got a call from a group that fit with your attitudes—perhaps a charity that supports the families of kids with cancer. If you said "no," the likely reason is that you were engaged with some other project, and you just didn't want to think about something else at that time.

This is the problem with interruption marketing. Even those who might be interested at some time are rarely interested at the time marketers interrupt them. This is no diatribe against telemarketing. Telemarketing is merely an example of interruption marketing.

Some marketers claim that it's normal for at least part of your market not to know that they need your product. And it is. But "educational" marketing is no different from any other kind of marketing: It's much more effective when your audience is pulling the knowledge to them when needed than when you push it at them, regardless of need.

The data suggests that prospects are much more likely to respond favorably to messages if they are not required to change their train of thought to grasp them. When you intercept prospects already looking for answers to certain questions, and you give them the answers they are looking for, you are bound to be much more effective.

Event Marketing: Short Shelf Life vs. Long Shelf Life

A common practice in marketing is to hold events to announce a new product's marketing calendar, enlisting the lion's share of resources leading up to the event. Once all the work is done and all the materials are published, you forget about the last event and start working on the next one. It's reminiscent of magazine publishing.

At one time, James was editor in chief of *ComputerUser* magazine, a monthly tabloid-style magazine distributed in large markets across the United States. His team spent all month working on the publication. As soon as it was at the printer, they started working on the next one. The only time they worried about previous issues was when they needed to issue corrections, which was rare.

About halfway through James' tenure at *ComputerUser*, the company started a website that supported the print publication. It started simply by publishing content online and by adding daily columns from columnists such as James. This inaugural website predated blogs, but the concept was the same: It allowed moderated comments not just on the daily columns but on the magazine articles.

The publish-and-forget model didn't work too well once *ComputerUser* moved to the web. *ComputerUser* soon found out that the articles published needed regular updates as users commented and otherwise contributed alongside the community of readers of the publication. Eventually, the community influenced the print editorial calendar, making it much more responsive to what the readers of the website showed the most interest in.

This experience convinced James that web audiences differ in fundamental ways from print audiences—and that is the main point of James' book

Audience, Relevance, and Search: Targeting Web Audiences with Relevant Content, which he wrote with Frank Donatone and Cynthia Fishel. The difference can be summed up in the attitude of the audiences: Whereas print audiences lean back to consume the content you provide, web audiences lean forward to interact with the content you provide. This might seem like an obvious thing, but when you unpack it, it gives you a rich way of understanding how to better engage with digital audiences—because digital *marketing* content invites interaction, too. While very few people *engage* with your digital content (share it, comment on it, like it, etc.), everyone is clicking their way to every piece of content they see, which is far different than in traditional media, where the content is essentially curated for consumers once they open a magazine or choose the TV channel. In other words, nothing happens online unless you click a lot. A lot can happen on TV if you click once.

This difference makes the event marketer's publish-and-forget model untenable on the web. James' print publication was recycled the moment after people read it. (*ComputerUser*'s copy editor lined her bird cage with it.) Print periodicals are archived, but the vast majority of readers experience it only in the month it is printed. Unlike print, web assets are available to users long after they are published and need to be updated as the facts on the ground change.

When you publish and forget on the web, your old assets become clutter that gets in the way of the assets you are trying to promote. A lot of event marketing sites are shut down after the event is over, which is a complete waste of much of the equity the event produced with the audience. But if you manage to have the same site for related events, one year of regular events with their own sets of assets soon becomes an incoherent mess of vaguely related content. Fragmented sites become less useful and more expensive over time.

The way to avoid this mess is to develop a content strategy that enables you to build a coherent site from repeated events. Before you publish content, you must plan to maintain and add onto that content to create a coherent and more comprehensive site over time. You also must plan to archive content when it is no longer useful or timely. The best content management tools automate these activities.

Lest this all sound neat and tidy and easy to plan, we must remind you that the data sets we use to understand audience preferences and attitudes are imperfect collections—and those preferences change over time. Natural language is fraught with all kinds of ambiguities and vagueness. Because you can never know in advance exactly how your audience will interact with your content, you must adjust content after publishing. Unlike with print, you can progressively improve your web content to better fit the needs of your audience over time. This is the premise of Mike's book *Do It Wrong Quickly*, in which he explains how to fail faster in order to succeed more fully in the end.

What Is Content Marketing?

We've thrown around the term *content marketing*, but we need to flesh it out more deeply. Content marketing is a fairly simple concept, and we don't want to overcomplicate it. It is the natural extension of a simple truth: Content is what users of digital media consume. It's what they look for when they search for stuff. It's what they promote when they like and share items.

Traditional marketers sometimes struggle to understand content marketing because it is such a departure from what they're used to. They're used to crafting visually compelling messages and pushing them out through various channels. They're not used to crafting content that attracts the audience to come to a website and participate in a customer experience. They're not used to using audience data to learn what those experiences should be before crafting them.

In fact, many organizations challenge the whole concept of content marketing. Critics say that creating high-quality content can be expensive. (Correct.) They say that it's risky to spend all that money up front before you even know it will work. (Correct.) They say that most of the people who see your content marketing will never buy from you. (Correct.) And, therefore, that's why you shouldn't adopt content marketing. (Not so correct.)

It's human nature to be distrustful of something new; distrust has probably benefited the survival of the species because it keeps us from tasting any mushroom within reach. But just because you are new to content marketing doesn't mean that you should distrust it. Yes, content marketing can sometimes be expensive and risky, and it is true that most people who see your marketing won't buy from you. But isn't advertising expensive and risky at times? And don't most of the people who see your ads pass up the chance to buy from you?

It isn't the *model* of content marketing that is a problem; after all, it's the same model as for advertising. It's just that we subject the unfamiliar to far more scrutiny than we bestow on older ideas that we are used to. So, if you're a traditional marketer, before you dismiss content marketing, perhaps learning some of the hallmarks of the discipline (as detailed below) will help you embrace it—and some of the data that helps you along the way.

Content Marketing Starts with Creating Great Content

Your content must consist of compelling, audience-centric, findable, sharable stories. If you build it, they might not come. Content must be built with audience interest in mind so that they will find it and share it with their peers. Once built, it must be published and promoted. Content does not market itself.

You measure the effectiveness of content marketing according to how often it is used and shared.

Content Is Useful Only in Context

You can't just create content in a vacuum. In digital media, content is only as valuable as the number and quality of references to it (links, social shares, etc.). It is more useful if it builds on existing work than if it duplicates it. It is more useful still if it is built as part of a system of other content that answers specific questions in a several-step information journey. This is especially difficult for traditional marketers, who want to tell self-contained stories.

You measure how well connected content is, within its context, by performing link analysis.

CONTENT MARKETING: THE NEW NEW THING?

All the cool kids are doing it. Content marketing is the flavor of the week, so you need to jump on the bandwagon, too. But is content marketing really new? Not really.

Ever hear of the *Michelin Guide*? This venerable series of review guide books started as a giveaway from the French tire manufacturer to encourage driving to restaurants (thus stoking demand for replacement tires). That was in 1900.

Know how *soap operas* got their name? These daytime serials started on the radio. They were actually produced by the soap manufacturers themselves. That was in 1930.

Such forays into content marketing set the tone for what we can do today. Many companies have engaged in content marketing over the

Content Needs Information Paths

Chances are that your audience will choose a different path through your content than the path that you designed. That's to be expected. Digital media and books are not the same. In books, it is the *author's* story. The reader implicitly concedes this point and passively consumes the story according to the author's agenda. Digital media need not be consumed in such a linear fashion. The *digital* reader or viewer is in control. It's *their* story, and they're piecing it together from multiple sources on the fly. This fact vexes some traditional marketers because, like book authors, they are accustomed to crafting media to be consumed serially.

You measure and track users through your content to create experiences that align with *their* journeys.

Great Content Speaks Your Customer's Language

Because the audience builds their stories using multiple sources, you must use language that the audience understands. Though you want to tell *your* story, your story will not make sense in the context of the audience's story if you don't use common language. Coining your own terms can lead to jargon that's confusing to your audience. It's natural for marketers to desire unique trademarked names for their products, but when you need to explain too many words, your message loses its punch.

---

years, so content marketing isn't truly new. What is new is how much cheaper it is, thanks to digital marketing.

In the old days (around 2003), content marketing brought with it high printing, production, or manufacturing costs and mailing or other distribution costs. Email, websites, social media, and mobile devices have dramatically reduced those costs. It is still expensive to create high-quality content, but it doesn't cost an arm and a leg to get it in front of your digital audience. What this means, in practical terms, is that any marketer with a good idea can scrape together the budget to experiment with content marketing. But it means anyone with a bad idea can do this, too. And that's the point.

Content marketing isn't new. What's new is that distributing your content is now almost free, so content marketing is feasible with just about any budget. Even yours.

You learn the common language by conducting keyword research and by listening to social channels.

Content Marketing Requires a Publisher's Reputation

As in all other forms of publishing, credibility is the currency in the digital world. A sure way to gain credibility is through transparency. Not only must you publish the truth as openly as possible, you need to avoid hyperbole and other forms of exaggeration. This can be especially hard for some public relations professionals who are used to telling only the "good stories."

You can measure the credibility of your content by performing sentiment analysis and other forms of social listening.

Content marketing is emerging as the primary way many brands engage with audiences, to the degree that resisting content marketing has become a career-limiting decision. For example, only 12% of UK companies do *not* focus on content marketing.

OUTSIDE-IN MARKETERS AS DATA SCIENTISTS

Big data is having big effects on content marketing, nowhere more than in its ability to make sense of the complexity of human language. Most web content consists of unstructured text. Mining this text for meaning and relevance is what search engines do. Search engines provide you with what they think are the most relevant and meaningful experiences, based on your search keywords. Understanding those results is the primary clue outside-in marketers use to better understand audience intent. Search engines are giant *natural language processing* engines that produce an urban dictionary full of definitions of keywords based on how they are used in digital media. In a sense, search engines "understand" how we use natural language over time.

The clues from this natural language processing rarely lead to cut-and-dried answers but are analyzed as statistics. Outside-in marketers use the data to make decisions about information their target audiences are *most likely* to need. They provide the information in ways they think will be most useful to them. But, all things considered, multiple versions of the same information are equally likely to serve audience needs. This is where outside-in marketers become data scientists—by serving multiple versions of the same digital experiences randomly to their audiences and testing the results. The experiences that get the best results win.

Wrapping Up: From Inside-Out to Outside-In

It should be clear by now that outside-in marketing is a radical new way of engaging in marketing. Digital drops distribution costs of content to nearly zero, allowing just about anyone to play. But outside-in marketing's most striking aspect is its use of data to understand the audience. Data allows marketers to provide the content they need to solve the audience's problems and to answer their questions.

By providing excellent customer experiences, you gain their trust and develop loyalty. When your customers are loyal in this way, they become your best marketers, promoting your brand to their friends and followers.

It all starts with credible and compelling stories geared toward what customers need, not driven from some clever campaign conceived in a *Mad Men*-style smoke-filled room. In concept, it might seem simple, but

---

This technique, known as *A/B testing* or *multivariate testing*, yields performance data that provides an ever-more-clear picture of how to better serve the target audience. A/B testing pits one variant against another (A vs. B), while the more powerful multivariate testing allows hundreds or even thousands of possibilities to compete with each other for supremacy. Patterns that tend to yield better results can be used as shortcuts by other digital marketing teams within the organization. In this way, outside-in marketing can sometimes be thought of as a form of *machine learning*, where the inputs of the machine are the practices and the outputs are improved performance. As the machine gets ever better at detecting working patterns for the target audience, it "learns" to optimize digital assets over time.

The machine is not just an optimization engine, however. The machine is a prioritization engine. Every marketer is faced daily with a challenge to do more with less. That means continually examining the mix of activities and weeding out poor performers and building new ones in their place, based on the data. The market is constantly in flux, and a savvy marketer is continuously adjusting the mix to match shifting audience needs and business priorities. This kind of agility was not possible prior to digital marketing. Now it is table stakes.

---

in practice, transforming your environment to this new approach requires major cultural, process, and technological changes to your environment. The remainder of this book describes these transformations and the results that have been achieved along the way, starting with a deeper dive in content marketing in the next chapter.

BEN EDWARDS, ON HIS SKEPTICISM OF CONTENT MARKETING

At the time of this interview, Ben Edwards was the Vice President of Global Digital Marketing at IBM, and he's currently leading PayPal.com. (Full disclosure: He was also James' boss at IBM.)

How important is content marketing to IBM?

Frankly, I struggle a little bit with content marketing as an idea. I prefer to simply talk about marketing, which contains two things: data and engagement. The two are related: The more engagement, the more data; the more data, the more engagement. I don't know what to do with content marketing, but I do know the questions we need to ask as marketers:

- Who do we need to engage?
- How do we need to engage with them?

The *how* depends on the *who*. In a world of infinite choice, we need to give them the answers they need when they need them, amidst lots of competition for their time and attention. The most successful at this are those that both understand who to engage with and understand that they need to make engagement as self-service as possible.

Let me give you a couple of scenarios.

Scenario 1 is an existing and significant IBM customer, who has been with IBM for 30 or 40 years as part of an integrated account. In this case, you bring in your best people for an in-person meeting to develop the relationship—your best SMEs [subject-matter experts] to deliver personalized expertise, creativity, and innovation. Then support that with a digital experience. This approach requires content in a high-touch engagement, geared toward the client's particular needs.

Scenario 2 is a developer who needs to understand how to test an app on Cloud Azure within [IBM's] Bluemix® [a cloud software development environment]. She needs a low-touch, self-directed content experience. You might need to bring in a human being on the phone to help her better understand how the platform works. Give her trials and other offers in a slick self-service model available on her laptop. That's a very different content model than Scenario 1.

In each scenario, you focus on the user and the use case—the client or prospect need. The question is, how do we successfully engage with them, given who they are and where they are in their journeys? I'm a little suspicious of content marketing. All these new flavors of marketing are all just marketing. It's all about the same challenge: Move people through their journey and inspire loyalty. The promise of modern marketing is that we can acquire more data, automate our messages, and engage with you in the moment of your journey with some relevance to the next thing for you to do.

There's a tension between focusing on large-scale opportunities versus one-to-one marketing. In our book, we advise you to prioritize your efforts toward the opportunities that tend to produce the highest volume of leads or wins. Marketing to the individual is more about low-volume, high-touch engagement, what we might call "sales." How do you reconcile these apparently conflicting motivations?

I don't think they're mutually exclusive. Getting to one-to-one entails being able to scale. In search marketing, as you know, you focus on the purchase intent implied by the keyword. This is a customer acquisition model. [As a prospect], once you're in my flow, I'm trying to understand how I can market to you as an individual, or some proxy of an individual. Take some high-volume keyword phrase. We've determined that 200,000 people are looking for that solution. Now you hit the site, and we can begin marketing to you in different ways than [we can to] that aggregate number. Maybe we can discover that that individual who downloads a particular asset has a 30% likelihood of buying. As soon as they download that asset, some other piece of data says, "Look, give them a call because they're ready to buy."

Content marketing can mean so many things, and IBM has so many offerings. Is there a philosophy that you bring to content marketing that somehow crosses all these languages, offerings, and styles?

Back up again and talk about marketing and not content marketing. We need a model of the individual at a moment in time, in the context of the account, of the company relationship, of their role in the purchase decision. And we need a model of the individual and the account as they move through time. It needs to model in a way that shows the value of the relationship for the individual and for IBM. The model measures value in terms of responses, leads, and wins.

The best way to learn the value of content is to focus on the offer. Offers have to provide value to people: Buy one, get one free; 30-day free trial, etc.—tangible value that simultaneously qualifies me as a purchaser, as a buyer. An offer is a marketing tactic of sufficient value to qualify the response. Good offers make it a high-quality response. The rest of marketing is customer acquisition, which is just getting more and more people to qualify for those offers.

The cornerstone of content value is the offer. [IBM's] SoftLayer® [cloud software] has a great offer—30-day free trial. How often do they change that offer? Never. TD Ameritrade has a great offer. They'll give you $600 to open a new account. They tried all kinds of other social content marketing without such an attractive offer. They spent millions on a social content marketing platform. The ROI on the $600 offer was better than all the social content marketing that they did. TD Ameritrade decided it is going to go back to traditional roots—to focusing on a great offer. The rest is all about how do I improve the flow of people to that offer? Social. Email. Search optimization. Etc.

I'll give you an example from B2B: the IBM Power® server line. When you buy one of these high-end servers, you make a large commitment. If I buy *one* of these boxes, I'm going to buy *a lot* of them. It's going to take you a fairly long time to convince me to buy one. Our data says that the tactic that converts to a quality response is a webinar, which is a two-hour time commitment. The thinking is, if I'm already making a serious time commitment in figuring out what server line to buy into, I can put two hours on my calendar. That webinar qualifies me for the next step, which is to start working with the sales organization.

So the question then is, "How do we improve the flow of qualified people into that webinar?" We provide lots of free learning content. We build lots of content to help them understand and compare—ROI calculators and TCO (Total Cost of Ownership) calculators, lots of thought leadership, social chats. I can imagine a whole ecosystem of engagement that gets people to that webinar. For that product and that buyer, most of the content effort is just getting people to the webinar.

When it comes to SoftLayer, the experience is frictionless. The offer brings people in without a lot of content up front. But marketing has to work a lot harder once we have you. For SoftLayer, retention is the harder nut to crack. The webinars for SoftLayer happen post purchase. Acquisition is relatively easy. Getting them to *try* is easy. Moving them from *try* to *buy* is tougher. Moving them from *buy* to *stay with us*—that's really tough. All the content heavy lifting for SoftLayer is about inspiring loyalty.

Those are two entirely different content models for two entirely different individuals.

It's not just about the technology, right? It's also a new way to manage people, no?

We are hacking the workflow through agile methods applied to unconventional development areas, such as marketing design systems. This whole [IBM] Studio we sit in is a petri dish of rapid application development. Teams move in, teams move out. Players within teams swap in and out. The backlogs are as fluid as the business requirements in a rapidly developing marketplace. The buzz here is palpable. Can you feel it?

The value of marketing is about investing in the right code and getting the right code to the right people at the right time—toward perpetual transformation—that's how management needs to transform itself, to evolve. That's what software is, especially in the age of cloud—perpetual improvement or dying. This facility is a physical manifestation of that.

It comes down to the question "Is marketing an expense or an asset?" In the old world, we gave agencies money to produce some work. The new model is, if you invest $1 in the platform, the platform becomes more powerful. You invest $35 million, and you get a whole lot better platform. We are proving that marketing is an asset. The platform is an asset. The Acquire–Engage–Convert model improves over time as we invest in it. Our data is proving that even as we continuously transform ourselves.

2

Content Marketing: A Deeper Dive

It was a tricky situation. We all want to lead with content marketing, but how do you do that when no one knows what your product is?

A company that shall remain nameless for reasons that will become obvious was looking for a solution to a problem that it felt imperiled its very existence. This national telephone company, which had recently been privatized from its previous government ownership, was suddenly concerned about a competitor its new owners kept asking about: Google.

Google sells ads to small businesses, and those businesses no longer want to be listed in the Yellow Pages, which is bad news for our heroes. What, they asked, can we do to convince small businesses that this is a mistake? How do we show that this is a fad? How can we scare those small businesses about the risk and expense associated with digital marketing?

Nervously, our team tried to proceed with our original proposal to them. We tried to explain how they had big advantages over Google. Yes, Google had an interesting ad product to sell, but how would Google reach all of those small businesses? This telco not only had the contact information (yes, phone numbers) for every small business in their country but it had "feet on the street"—a sales force that no competitor could match. We breathlessly proposed how they could partner with our agency services to offer a website to every small business for not much more than they paid for a full-page ad.

You can guess the outcome. That's why we won't reveal the name of the company.

The point of the story is that no matter what message the telco wanted to convey to its customers, it needed content marketing. It needed to educate its market that change is in the winds and that you need us now. But they would have had a lot easier time focusing on a message that would really help their customers rather than on one that was designed to feather their own decaying nest.

And that is what we tackle in this chapter: what content marketing is and, just as importantly, what it is not.

What Content Marketing Is

At its base, content marketing provides the content your audience needs. Content marketing can be entertaining, helpful, or informative, or perhaps it can help solve your audience's problem. One good test of content marketing is whether it helps your audience even if they never buy your product or service.

If by now you are starting to wonder if content marketing will test your abilities, you should know that it doesn't need to be complex. IT managed services provider Logicalis took the simple step of providing a free ebook that explained how companies using today's technologies to run their data centers can be ready for the changes that cloud computing and other technical trends have in store.

Logicalis didn't set out to sell anything (although, obviously, they *wanted* their marketing to result in sales). They just tried to be helpful, to explain what they thought their customers needed to know so that their customers could be successful. It was a classic "thought leadership" campaign, which is one of the basic techniques in content marketing. The results? In just three months, $8 million in added revenue closed or in the pipeline.

One of the reasons that Logicalis was so successful is that its information is credible, which is the first characteristic of content marketing.

Content Marketing Is Credible

In order for content marketing to be helpful or informative, it needs to be credible. Rather than using the kind of breathless hype that characterizes most sales pitches, content marketing needs to set a tone closer to that of a newspaper article or a trade magazine—or even a documentary. It must show, not tell. It must advise, not sell. It must enrich rather than pitch.

When your marketing is credible, you begin to build a relationship with your audience based on trust. When you gain their trust, you can influence their buying decisions. The more trustworthy your content experiences, the more effective your content marketing becomes.

As with much of content marketing, it sounds simple, but it is tempting to cram in a little bit about your product, right? Don't.

Your audience has a finely tuned BS filter. (BS stands for blatant sales. No, really.) When that filter goes off, they stop listening. They start questioning whether the information is for your benefit or theirs. You lose trust.

Some successful content marketing can be entertaining—much of consumer marketing works that way—but content marketing is more often applied to high-consideration products, such as technology products or business services, that require lots of information and a long sales cycle.

The credibility of your information is essential to gaining trust. If you provide enough helpful information, you establish your company as the expert in the field. When you clearly describe the problem that needs to be solved and you help solve it, your credibility goes sky high, and customers begin to believe that you are the answer to their prayers.

While some members of your audience will be able to consume your content and solve their problems on their own, enough of them will be unable or unwilling to tackle the problem on their own—and that's why they engage your products or services to do the job.

Instead of using marketing that puts the product front and center, why not try an approach that puts the customer first?

Freightliner, the largest division of Daimler Trucks North America, wanted to help its largest group of customers, individual owner-operators—the drivers who own their own truck rather than get paid by a large company to drive a truck. Instead of blanketing this audience with boatloads of content on why they should buy a new truck, Freightliner realized that their customers' biggest challenge was that they were now running a business, not just driving a truck. So they put together the Team Run Start online community and loaded it up with the very advice that owner-operators needed.

What kind of advice, you ask? Everything truckers need to know about their trucks. About fuel economy—one of their biggest costs. About the business of trucking—because these owner-operators own their own business, too. And about their health—because sitting in a truck all day brings its own unique health issues.

This content obviously struck a chord with the target audience, attracting 18,000 members in two years. These members now have a very different relationship with Freightliner than they did before. What do you think the odds are that at least a few of these people buy a Freightliner truck the next time they are in the market?

Content Marketing Is Targeted

Most successful marketing is targeted, so it isn't surprising that content marketing is, also. You can target your content marketing by using traditional targeting approaches, with demographics (for B2C marketers) or firmographics (for B2B businesses)—such as industry or company size. But content marketing typically employs deeper targeting than other kinds of marketing, employing finer-grained techniques, such as these:

- *Personas.* Far more specific than market segments, personas include motivations and psychographics that could include even particular content factors, such as learning style. If your target persona has an experiential learning style, for example, you might tend toward games, videos, webinars, and other more interactive fare rather than blog posts and newsletters.

- *Stages of the buyer's journey.* Someone who is just learning about a problem is not ready for a coupon. Your content needs to be carefully targeted based on where the buyer is in the journey to a purchase.

- *Message resonance.* You can target a message to an individual at the right stage in the buy cycle, but it still might not resonate. How do you know it is doing its job (i.e., helping the client or prospect take the next step in her journey)? A/B testing and multivariate testing allow you to identify effective messages—not just in general but when targeted to specific personas within a stage of the buyer's journey.

In the past, marketing messages were targeted at archetypes—such as housewives, dads, executives, or line-of-business managers. Now we can market to individuals—for example, a finance officer of a particular company—giving them all and only the content they need, when they need it. Search is the main way we accomplish this, but social shares, emailing links, and other methods provide information specially selected for the recipient. It's the marketer's job to provide the right content in the first place. In this way, we can build trust with customers faster and have stronger influence over their brand and buying preferences.

Content Marketing Is Differentiated

How do you build messages that tend to help your audience take the next step in their client journeys? One question that comes up throughout the buyer's journey is "How can your company help me solve my problems better than your competitors?"

Before you answer that question, you need to understand what marketers mean when they talk about *differentiation* because most marketers don't understand this concept very well. Most marketers believe that differentiation is about how their product or service is *different* from their competitors' offerings. And it is. But it's more than that.

Differentiation is a difference that a market will *pay* for.

Let that roll around in your head for a minute. *Every* product is different. Unless you are selling a complete commodity, your product is different in *some* way. You need to truly focus on a difference for your product that at least part of your audience values enough to shell out their hard-earned cash.

GoPro, the runaway hit camera that can record people doing just about anything, knew what its differentiation was from the start: It could take videos that no other camera could. So it began with surfers, but it quickly expanded into other sports by marketing with its best possible content—videos posted by its thrilled customers. Because their customers understood GoPro's differentiation, the company rarely heard objections such as "I already have a camera" or "I can use my phone as a camera" because GoPro was focused tightly on customers who could not get these shots any other way. GoPro never fooled themselves by going after a market that any existing camera competed in. They created a completely differentiated space for themselves and stuck with content marketing that sold the product in an utterly convincing way.

Most people, however, don't realize how long GoPro stuck with that differentiation. The company started with a 35mm film camera and didn't even introduce a digital camera for three years—in 2005. Each successive year, technology improvements broadened GoPro's appeal, but their focus on a differentiated market survived every technology change. Differentiation is not something you can change with each new marketing campaign; it must be woven deep into your offering.

You need to approach your content marketing the same way, but it takes some bravery. We are all tempted to market our offerings as broadly as possible. We'd love to think that every possible prospect out there should buy what we are selling. And, to be sure, if someone wants to buy your product, no matter who they are, go ahead and sell it. But that isn't how you market it.

Can you imagine if GoPro tried to market its camera to all photographers? No one would have figured out what their true differentiation was, so their ideal audience might never have found them. Yes, there are more generic camera buffs than the folks who buy GoPros, so you might have said, "Let's try to be a little broader here," but that would have been a colossal error. It takes bravery, but you must be focused on that small segment that you are differentiated for when you start your content marketing.

Another way to say it is that you need to be very focused on that segment of your audience who would be absolute idiots not to buy from you. You start your content marketing by identifying that segment and isolating the specific problems that group has—problems different from other segments. These are the problems that your offering solves better than any competitor: That is true differentiation.

Focusing your initial content marketing efforts on content that describes and addresses these problems is your best approach because if you can't persuade *those* buyers with your content marketing, you sure aren't going to persuade anyone else.

Because differentiation is so important, marketers tend to make a crucial mistake: They focus on "how we're different" *too* much. In the process, they lose sight of the market. Clients and prospects are in the market for something that solves their problems or fulfills a need. They express those things in their own terms, which tend to be in the common parlance of the market. Differentiation makes sense to them only relative to that common parlance. If you try to be clever and use words to describe your differentiation that don't make sense within the common parlance, your differentiation won't work. Mainstream customers worry about products they can't compartmentalize in some way.

It's a fine line. And you really don't know what level of differentiation will resonate with your audience until you try different levels and see what works. GoPro wasn't an overnight success. They had to experiment. In experimenting, they found that their product had a broader appeal to more than just surfers. So they built that into their differentiated messaging.

If you're wondering where to start, differentiation is a good place. But the important thing is starting. Do your homework. Take your best shot. And prepare to adjust as necessary.

Content Marketing Is Measurable

The fundamentals of content marketing haven't changed. The medium has. The digital medium enables all kinds of analyses of the target audience. Fine-grained analysis can be used to target the audience not only with the content they need but in the time and space that is most convenient to them.

That's the theory, anyway. The practice is quite a bit more complex. The types of data we use to learn audience preferences are many and varied. Data comes at us at alarming speed, and it accumulates in huge volumes. The *big data* that content marketers need to use can be intimidating, especially to traditional marketers, but it can be summarized into four hallmarks—known as the four *V*s:

- *Volume.* This is the "big" part, but you probably knew that.
- *Velocity.* This extreme speed of incoming data has never been seen before.
- *Variety.* You have structured data coming from your metrics analysts in spreadsheet form. You have unstructured data coming from your keyword research and social listening, which starts out as plain text. You have A/B test data. You have user experience studies. You have surveys. It all comes together to produce meaning in different ways.
- *Veracity.* None of this matters unless you know you have accuracy.

Because this is a book about content marketing and big data, it isn't enough to just make the claim that content marketing is measurable. We need to go deeper, into exactly what kind of metrics a successful content marketer needs. Some metrics, called *structured data*, belong in spreadsheets and relational (i.e., SQL) databases. But many modern metrics are derived from unstructured data—text, images, videos, and other kinds of data that is more complex to analyze than rows of numbers and values. We call it big data not just because there is a lot of it but because analysis of it involves mixing both structured and unstructured data.

Let's look at the many kinds of big data that content marketers need to analyze.

Search Keywords

You learn the language of your audience by conducting search keyword research. Regardless of your audience, they will primarily start their information journeys with search. And the more complex the problem or information challenge, the more likely they will use search throughout their information journey. Mining this activity will give you a good sense of the topics they're interested in. If you do it right, you can also learn the questions customers ask and the problems they want to solve. Once you have a good sense of the keywords your audience uses in search, you can plug these keywords into social listening tools to learn even more words they use when they write about these topics in social settings. In this way, you can learn the language that resonates with your audience.

Social Listening

You can measure the credibility of your content by using sentiment analysis and other analytics applied to social media conversations. The same tools that mine the language of your audience in social settings can also measure their emotions and the intensity of those emotions. How positive or negative are they about the topic when they post in social settings? How do they feel about your content? Comments on your content, especially in social media, can also be powerful places for listening.

Social Endorsements

If your audience thinks highly enough of your content to actually *share* it to their friends and followers—by retweeting it, sharing it on Facebook, or taking equivalent actions on other social networks—it shows a high degree of relevance and credibility. Another kind of lesser endorsement is a Like on Facebook, a Twitter Favorite, or a similar action on other social platforms.

Links

Another type of endorsement is a link from another content owner to your page. You can measure the connections to your content by performing link analysis to measure the number and the credibility of links to your content. The other content owner then works with their media relations colleagues to try to close any gaps in the interwoven information between their information and their media partners. They also work with their own development teams to strengthen link relevance between the content on their pages and related pages.

Search Referrals

Search referrals count how many searchers have clicked on your content from a search engine's results page. Although in recent years search engines and web browsers have been blocking the actual keyword data related to these referrals, you can still get raw counts of referrals that tell you how many people Google or Bing sent to your site. Of course, people don't click your listings in search engines if you don't rank well for important keywords. So referrals are a function of *ranking* and how well your snippet (the words underneath the title on the results page) entices searchers to click. Because Google and other search engines are trying to list the most relevant content for a searcher's keyword, ranking is a good indicator of relevance. Referrals are even better because referrals mean that the quality of your page's snippet was good enough to attract a click.

Social Referrals

Social referrals are indicators of how well regarded your content is in the marketplace of ideas. Social referrals indicate how many people have followed links to your content shared in social media. People don't share content unless they value it, and the recipients don't click shared items unless they trust the endorsement of their social connection.

Bounces

Once someone lands on your content, the central question is whether it meets their needs, which some might call relevance. You can measure content relevance with a metric called *bounce rate*. A visitor who clicks the Back button deems the content irrelevant—and that's a *bounce*. A visitor who clicks the links you provide deems the content at least marginally relevant.

Paths

When your audience does click your links, what paths do they take? You might design paths through your content, but your audience will tell you to what extent they think your paths make sense. You can track users through your content to see what journeys make the most sense to them. This information can help you make your content experiences more effective over time.

Conversions

Beyond bounces, if visitors to your site go so far as to buy your product or to request to be contacted by sales, that can be counted as a *conversion*. Counting conversions is the first step in showing the value of your marketing with ROI for increased sales.

If big data feels a bit intimidating, we understand. Most marketers went into marketing as a refuge from math, but unfortunately, the numbers have caught up with you. It's not necessary that you be the person actually crunching the numbers, but you need to be willing to make decisions *based* on the numbers rather than on your golden gut. We'll try to make this as easy a transition as possible.

What Content Marketing Is Not

Like any other emerging field, content marketing has its share of detractors, and they often have a point. Let's walk through some of the wrong ways to approach content marketing so that you can avoid these mistakes in your own marketing.

Content Marketing Is Not About Volume

Mark Schaefer recently coined the phrase *content shock* to describe the impending cliff of despair facing content marketers. The theory says content marketers produce so much stuff that the practice will eventually collapse under its own weight, as audiences tune out the crushing volume of content. Technically, the theory is based on the simple economics of supply and demand. As supply grows, the price for goods goes down. But because content marketers give their stuff away for free, content marketing is not sustainable. The content will eventually reach a negative value, causing more harm than good.

The main myth we want to bust relative to content shock is that content is free. Content is never free. The audience might not pay for it in money, but they pay for it with time and attention. It has to have at least enough value to be worth the time and attention of the audience. Because audience time and attention become more precious with each passing day, high-quality content will continue to gain in relative value against its lower-quality competition. High-quality content differentiates companies from their competitors.

Content quality is a hallmark of content marketing. You can't build trust with your audience unless you build quality content. Of course, this is easier said than done. But here again we can use data to measure how well our content performs for our target audiences and make adjustments as we go. It might not be perfect when it is published, but using big data can improve the content over time and make it a competitive advantage.

Another aspect of content shock is that audiences are drowning in content. Whether or not you believe Schaefer's theory about the economics of content marketing, the practice tends to overwhelm the audience if it is not done right. But this also is nothing new. Information on the web has grown exponentially since the web's debut in 1994, and it continues to grow at a rapid clip even 20 years after its inception, as shown in Figure 2-1.

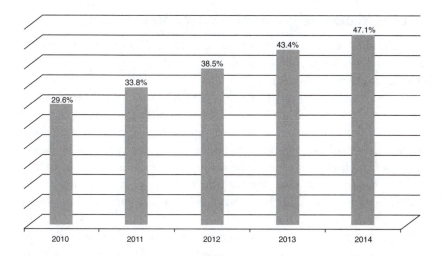

Figure 2-1   Each year, the percentage of time that U.S. adults spend with digital media increases.
Source: eMarketer

Users have adapted to the crushing volume of content on the web by being more proactive about the information they consume. Primarily, users *search* for what they're looking for rather than passively consume information from just a few trusted sources. And this search behavior is much more interactive than with other media, in part because much of what people find on the web is marginally relevant to their searches. Because Google and other search engines do a great job of finding the right content for searchers, delivering appropriate content for your audience is much more important than delivering high volumes of content.

Other algorithms complement search as a means of filtering the enormous volume of content on the web. Building content with these algorithms in mind is a key differentiator. For example, you can use tools to discover which of your pages rank in Google or other search engines for the keywords your target audience queries. If you rank, it is a good indicator that your content is doing the job. Rather than publish more stuff that competes with ranking pages, find areas or topics where you don't rank and build or optimize *that* content.

If you fill all the gaps in Google's search engine results with useful content and avoid needless duplication, you can minimize content shock. In this way, algorithms can help you publish only the content you need to publish and continually optimize the content you have already published.

Content Marketing Is Not a Cheaper Form of Print

Besides the economic argument, content shock is based on a premise that need not be true—that all content marketers publish way too much content for their audiences to consume.

It is true that many companies publish entirely too much content. A common practice is to find an audience need and publish the content that meets that need prior to seeing if something similar has already been published on your site. Especially in big companies, communication and collaboration about published content can be scarce. The result is a lot of apparently duplicate content competing for the time and attention of the target audience. Companies that find themselves in that predicament *do* run afoul of their audience's content shock.

But it need not be so. The growing content strategy field has built many handy tools to audit existing content and see to what extent it meets the needs of the target audience. Companies can either republish or optimize the content, collaborating with the original publishers to serve their mutual audiences. We call this practice *content governance*. The best content governance focuses on meeting the needs of clients and prospects rather than the needs of the marketer. If you meet client needs, results will follow. If you don't meet client needs, the reverse happens.

Along with SEO, content strategy and content governance are antidotes to content shock. But they, too, are not in traditional marketers' comfort zones. Content audits can be complex documents, laced with metrics and unstructured data to help companies determine which content to retire, which content to update or optimize, and which content to create and publish.

Just as marketers can employ data scientists to help make sense of the effectiveness of their content marketing, marketers can use content strategists to digest all the audits. And they should do so, enabling traditional marketers to focus on learning their audience and serving audience needs.

Content Marketing Is Not Merely Social Media Marketing

Another common aspect of content marketing is its inherently social nature. Content marketers are known for promoting blogging as a form of customer engagement. Blogs are inherently social, focusing on authors and the connections they have with their friends, followers, and colleagues. This means building author influence by growing their reach within social networks such as Twitter and LinkedIn.

It can be a very successful way of engaging with customers, in part because social media is a key way users find content on the bloated web. Users search for content in areas in which they are not experts. But for their areas of expertise, they tend to use their social connections to grow their expertise. Enabling your internal experts to build this content helps clients and prospects deeply engage with your brand.

For some, the success of social media marketing leads to the conclusion that it should replace the content on websites. We were recently in a room full of executives discussing how to transform the marketing practices of a large enterprise, when an executive said, "Websites are dead; we should create all our content in social networks, where our clients can connect with our experts." We cautioned that the distinction between content on the corporate website and content in social settings is a bit artificial. They are both social in nature. They both should feature experts and expertise. But the website, not social networks, is where clients convert. Social networks have their place as neutral meeting and sharing grounds. But they cannot replace corporate websites.

Even if somehow you become convinced that a particular social site is a good replacement for your website, you *still* shouldn't switch. Why? It's just too risky. If you think that Tumblr should be your ultimate destination and Tumblr someday closes, you're screwed. (Even if it doesn't close, try getting a Tumblr site to rank well in Google. Google doesn't index Tumblr content.) If you promote Facebook as your ultimate destination and Facebook later changes the rules, you might find that you no longer can use Facebook the way you expected.

Your marketing website is the destination to which you attract and convert clients. Social sites are important, and we will discuss them at greater length later. But unless you learn to optimize your site to convert your prospects into loyal clients, who come to it from social channels, social media will serve only as a branding tool. The two must work together as a cohesive whole to maximize the value of your social efforts. These efforts are among the most difficult things to do as you attempt to transform your marketing organizations. Your website can be a proving ground for what works and what doesn't in social media. Without a strong web presence, social media is a waste of your most precious resources—your experts.

Content Marketing Is Not Merely Online Publishing

One of the first things we tell clients when we advise them to adopt content marketing is to accept the fact that they are publishers. Effectively managing their publishing process is a key differentiator for content marketers. Initially, many of our clients think that all they need to do is to build the project plans for their campaigns to push out content.

By all means, editorial calendars are useful things, but they should not be seen as the be-all and end-all of content marketing management. The trouble with paying too much attention to an internal editorial calendar is in the word *push* you probably noticed in the previous paragraph. Pushy content marketing is not particularly effective, and it is very expensive.

In our experience, the messaging at the center of push marketing changes rapidly, and the marketers who are eager to push the message out will publish reams of content. Unless the basis of the message offers new value—such as a new product launch—in the eyes of the audience, the message is not that different from the previous pushy thing published. Besides wasting the time of the folks who create and manage the content, this flavor of content marketing wastes the most precious commodity to marketers—the time and attention of their audience—possibly encouraging the audience to tune out future messages. Then, like the boy who cried "wolf," push marketers don't get the attention they deserve when they publish something truly compelling.

Many of our clients start publishing the messages they want the market to hear rather than publishing the answers the market wants to know. Outside-in marketing focuses on publishing the content that clients and prospects need so that they will pay attention to the messages you need to publish.

If you think about it, focusing on the needs of your clients and prospects will help focus your development teams, your support teams, and other areas of your company around those needs. So, even though outside-in marketing starts with the needs of the customers, it ultimately results in published content that also meets the needs of the marketer.

Content Marketing Is Not Just for Market Capture

Traditional marketers speak often of *making* markets, establishing brands, and growing market share. Historically, this has been done by building compelling messages and pushing them into the markets. This practice remains both prevalent and effective, as a quick study of Apple's marketing strategy demonstrates.

What you might not know is that Apple constantly studies the needs of their audience before building the products that suit those needs. They design products that are so elegant and useful that they practically market themselves. But your company probably does not have the benefit of Apple's laser focus on client needs, so push marketing might not work as well for you.

For most companies, content marketing itself needs to be a differentiator. If you provide excellent experiences by giving your clients valuable information and access to your experts, you have a chance to develop a relationship with them based on trust. In the comfort of this trust, clients and prospects will give you their precious time and attention to learn your points of view and your unique value propositions. As we said, you can't do this with a push approach, at least not in digital.

You might ask, "If content marketing is primarily geared toward serving audience needs, how can you make markets with it?" Not only can you make markets, content marketing is perhaps the *most* effective way to make markets. As we said, a *loyal* audience is more receptive to your point of view (POV). As long as you provide compelling evidence and well-crafted stories, clients and prospects will more readily accept your POV after you have developed a relationship with them, built on trust. But they are less likely to accept your POV if they don't yet trust you.

Perhaps an example will help. James consulted internally with thousands of marketers in IBM, trying to help them make markets with outside-in content marketing. In 2013, one of those clients was IBM Research, which was attempting to make the market for cognitive computing, a new model of computing best exemplified by Watson, the computer that beat the top *Jeopardy!* champions. When he started working with IBM Research, they wanted to push the message of this new kind of computing to the marketplace but were struggling to convince skeptical researchers, primarily in academia, that this new model was as revolutionary as they claimed.

As is typical, James built a seed list of keywords from the existing marketing messages and then performed keyword research. What he found was that what IBM called "cognitive computing" was being searched for by academic audiences with keywords such as *artificial intelligence, natural language processing,* and *machine learning.* His team built a periodic table of cognitive computing that included all of these popular words, with some annotations about how they related. He then advised the team to build content around each of the squares in the periodic table and build an experience that linked the content together in a coherent way.

The content they created helped people who searched for *artificial intelligence* and related words to understand the similarities and differences between these popular practices and cognitive computing. Once the site helped the audience understand these things, it conditioned the conversation toward the view that cognitive computing is not the same as traditional artificial intelligence but that it is much more sophisticated. It also told compelling stories about how cognitive computing systems are helping doctors, scientists, and others do amazing things they could never do without cognitive computing.

This content helped IBM Research make the market for cognitive computing. Prior to the content being published, there were five monthly U.S. searches containing the words *cognitive computing,* according to Google. Six months after publishing, there were 1,400 U.S. monthly searches containing that same phrase. By using the audience's language, peppered with IBM's POV, IBM Research made the market for cognitive computing. IBM Research did not buy one ad to drive traffic to the content it created. It made the market for cognitive computing by capturing the market for related words.

Content Marketing Is Not a Replacement for Public Relations

Content marketing is a particularly effective kind of digital marketing, but it is not the only way to provide answers to your clients and prospects. Advertising still plays a role. And you still need to engage in traditional public relations (PR). Rather than view content marketing as a replacement for traditional PR, as some have recommended, we believe both must work together.

According to a recent study by Nielsen, PR is 88% more effective than content marketing alone. Though the poll respondents frequently used expert advice from companies, journalistic content from third-party publishers is still the most effective consumer influencer.

Convincing reputable publishers to review your products or to mention your brand in favorable ways is an art that we will leave to media relations books. Just as with data scientists and content strategists, traditional marketers should delegate this art to those who specialize in PR. But that doesn't mean you don't work with them to craft a united front between your internal and external experts.

In particular, marketers must inform PR professionals about related content marketing activities so that PR people can build them into their press releases and other media relations assets. What the Nielsen study did not test is whether media relations assets are more effective in getting favorable mentions if they include good links to credible content marketing assets by your experts. The study pitted the two practices against each other rather than considering the two practices in concert.

Wrapping Up: Content Marketing Takes a Village

By now you are getting the idea that content marketing includes practices that are often treated as their own disciplines, including:

- Content strategy
- Public relations
- Corporate publishing
- Search marketing
- Social media marketing

Content marketing integrates these practices into one unified, governed whole. Indeed, your success or failure in content marketing will depend largely on how well you integrate data and these other disciplines to create excellent customer experiences. If you don't integrate your practices and your applications, turf wars and other corporate nastiness will turn your content marketing efforts into an out-of-control publishing house that overwhelms your audience.

It doesn't have to be that way.

In upcoming chapters, we describe how to integrate these disciplines into a cohesive, governed unit devoted to providing your audience with the helpful information they are seeking—and reaching your own marketing goals in the process. Next, in Chapter 3, we tackle a key transformation your company needs to succeed in content marketing: your culture.

MARK SCHAEFER EXPLAINS "CONTENT SHOCK"

Mark Schaefer blogs at {grow}, is a keynote speaker, consults, teaches at the college level, and is the author of several best-selling marketing books, including Social Media Explained.

Tell marketers why they need to understand "content shock."

In each phase of Internet development, it gets more difficult for marketers as the space matures.

For example, if you were the first business in your industry with a website, you certainly had an advantage until your competitors caught on. Similarly, with SEO, if you were the first to rise to the top of the search rankings, you were winning until your cost to stay at the top increased exponentially as competitors figured it out.

The same thing is happening now as the social media/content marketing space matures. We are being faced with an explosion of new content, all competing for consumer attention. What worked a few years ago, or even a few months ago, may not work now.

At the same time, consumer attention span is limited. They will be more discerning in what they consume; they will demand more relevance and higher quality, pushing up the cost to compete.

They will also be employing advanced filters meant to keep new messages out. Good for them, but challenging for marketers!

We are certainly at a time when marketers need to reconsider their direction on digital strategy every few months. There is no such thing as an annual plan anymore.

So experts have finally sold marketers on the idea that content is more authentic, deeper, more credible, and cheaper than other forms of marketing. How does a newly minted content marketer avoid shocking the audience?

There is no blanket answer to the issue of standing out in a world of increasing information density. It is highly dependent on the competitive circumstances of your industry. For example, some niches may still be devoid of helpful content, representing a ripe opportunity for a marketer.

However, in a crowded niche, you will certainly have to do something more strategic than simply pumping out blog posts or videos. You will need to examine your ability to maneuver very carefully. Can you create different types of content? Target an underserved audience? Use promotion or distribution in a more skillful way? Dominate a certain platform? You can't simply create an advantage by copying a competitor. You need to have a thoughtful and unique response, or your results will be disappointing.

It sounds like content shock certainly applies to outbound content marketing—the stream of newsletters, blog posts, tweets, and other things that get shipped when produced. Can content shock apply when someone is searching for information?

Absolutely. Consumers can become absolutely paralyzed by the amount of information out there. In fact, retailers have observed a condition where people spend so much time researching a product that they never actually purchase. They know that information with "the right answer" is out there, and they search and search because they feel guilty not having the perfect answer.

If it is true that content marketers publish way more content than their audiences can consume, will it still be true when the access to that content is personalized to each audience member?

Five years ago, when you or I did a search on Google for the best deal on an automobile or a review of a new car model, we would get similar results...probably the *same* results. But over time, Google has made its search results highly tailored to you and your environment. Where are you? Who are you? Who are your friends? This has resulted in an ever-tightening bubble of personalized results. The results you get today are almost certainly different than what I get.

An advanced content filter such as Zite is an even more extreme example of this because it actually pushes content to you and only you, constricting the scope of possible content that you see. Let's say that you are trying to create content about automobiles that will be organically discovered by a high-potential customer like me. To get through this filter, you won't just have to somehow push it to the top of Google, you may also have to get it through the Zite algorithm—and all the Zite competitors crowding into this increasingly important space. [Editor's note: Zite was acquired by Flipboard and shut down after this interview.]

Will that require different strategies? Perhaps we won't just be concerned with SEO. We might also need to consider Zite Engine Optimization. This new era of mega-filters will also present a challenge to any organization or brand trying to introduce a new idea or product. Today, when I read an online newspaper or news feed, I am also presented with many alternative content choices. This content might be well out of my normal comfort zone but interesting to me nonetheless.

But as information density increases in my busy world, I can see the day when I will spend almost all my time with my own personalized filter. I would rarely see things outside my comfort zone because keeping me *in* my comfort zone is exactly what these filters are trying to do! If Zite figures out I'm politically liberal, it is probably not going to offer an editorial with a conservative viewpoint. That would be a "filter fail."

Every online organization is collecting data about us, determining what we are going to view and hear, based on the stereotype they are creating for us.

Is content marketing still the "next big thing" (or the current big thing)? Or do you see something better coming along for marketers to pay attention to?

Content in some form has always been the centerpiece of marketing and always will be. I think that what is next is new forms of content (3D, augmented reality, immersive), the distribution of the content in an era of information density, and the discovery of content that is critical for marketers to consider going forward.

It was rather elegant many years ago to be limited in our content distribution options—three network TV stations (in America at least), some local radio stations, and some newspapers and magazines. The future of marketing from here on out is breaking through the cacophony of a million channels to become the signal instead of the noise.

3

Content Marketing Transformation: Culture

There was a kind of awkward silence. It was the moment when they suddenly realized that this wasn't a technical problem or a marketing problem. It was a culture problem.

We were sitting in a beautiful conference room with the top marketing team of a luxury automaker. Their original concern was that their dealers were at each other's throats, overextending their digital marketing reach beyond their agreed-to territories. But it soon became clear that there were more important issues.

As is common with car manufacturers, the marketing team fiercely protected the mother brand. Dealers were not allowed to advertise anything about the brand image, and so the dealer ads skewed more to actors dressing as George Washington because they can't tell a lie about their President's Day sales event. But with the advent of the Internet, dealers discovered that content marketing was possible for all sorts of purposes—everything from the "no-pressure sales experience" to getting new car quotes by email to a service "club" that picks up your car from your house.

The automaker's marketing team started to realize that these kinds of marketing campaigns might actually have more of an impact on the consumer's view of their brand than their national ad campaign. But how would they get back control of their brand image? The dealers were operating within the prescribed culture around the national vs. local advertising rules.

And that's a big part of what this chapter is about—the changes required in your culture to adopt outside-in marketing. Large companies tend to consider culture in their strategies more than smaller ones, but as the luxury automaker teaches us, cultures exist even across companies in whatever ecosystem of large and small companies make up your marketing and sales channels. And controlling the brand is not the real problem for the automaker; that is inside-out thinking.

How do you transform a marketing organization to become more outside-in? Often the first hurdle is creating a culture centered on excellent customer experiences.

Assuming that (at best) marketing budgets are static each year, digital transformation requires convincing executives to transfer money from push

USING THE CUSTOMER'S LANGUAGE

One of James' favorite projects at IBM involved working with the Smarter Planet® content team to help them craft more outside-in content. Officially, his role was search engine optimization, but he saw his job as much more elemental—not focused on just optimizing pages but on helping teams craft content that resonates with the target audience.

One topic within Smarter Planet was called Smarter Water®. It was about how IBM uses big data and analytics to help governments and NGOs better manage the Earth's most precious resource. It was fun for James not only because it is a topic he is passionate about but because the stories were very compelling. When you can show how better water management technology can give an entire small city access to clean drinking water for the first time, the story practically writes itself.

James' small contribution to the content marketing for Smarter Water was to add the word *management* to the end of the topic. It might seem like the tiniest change, but it had a huge and immediate effect. You see, Smarter Water was a new topic, with practically nonexistent search or social conversation volume. But water *management* was a huge and growing topic in both search and social spheres—for obvious reasons. It was the umbrella topic for all the ways in which governments and municipalities treat wastewater and provide clean water for their constituents. It also contains an environmental component as well.

marketing to pull marketing. To maximize the return on these new pull investments, you must transform the culture of the organization to be more client focused. As clients repeatedly express their preference for messages on and in their terms, the organization will be forced to transform to a more outside-in approach.

Outside-in marketing is for marketers who want to grow their businesses as quickly as possible. To do so, you need new customers. The best way to attract and retain new customers is by getting messages in front of them, in their own language, when they are making purchasing decisions. If you use their language, you have a good chance of attracting them to your content when they're ready to take the next step in their purchase journey. If you build experiences that help them take that next step, without pushing them into it, you stand a chance to add them to your client list.

Because so many people were talking and searching on the topic, relaunching the topic as Smarter Water Management resulted in astronomical growth in traffic and engagement on the topic within IBM's Smarter Planet website. But the change also sent shock waves throughout the marketing and communications groups, serving as a catalyst to a chain reaction of culture change throughout the two organizations.

When IBM built the new Smarter Water Management topic, the team found a wealth of examples of IBM's long-standing work in this area. For example, IBM has helped the City of New York manage its water for years. Also, IBM research scientists are central to efforts to clean up the Hudson River. And there are many other stories from around the globe. Few of these stories were widely known at the time, but the collaborative effort turned some of these scientists into celebrities.

Much of this content was curated on the ibm.com Smarter Water Management topic, but some was left to connect audiences to the topic in blogs and other social settings outside the walls of ibm.com. All the media relations activity had the new name in it. Advertising used the new name. Even the IBM THINK® exhibit, which debuted at Lincoln Center in New York and now resides at Epcot Center at Disney World, had stories related to smarter water management. All this activity contributed to the growth in queries for *water management* and made Smarter Water Management a trending topic. One small change had a huge impact. This is the promise of outside-in marketing.

Culture Transformation Starts with Listening

Company executives love to claim that their corporate culture emphasizes *listening* to the customer. In traditional companies, the eyes and ears of the company are centered in three organizations: sales, customer support, and market research. Of course, these three organizations are valuable sources of listening data. But they should not be the sole sources. Transforming your culture to one of listening to the customer must become a part of every role in the company rather than be restricted to a few organizations.

Sales Listening

As we've said, we expect sales leaders to learn customer preferences. If anything, listening to what customers say has taken on new significance in recent years, given the rise in the importance of customer advocacy in attracting new customers to your product or service, as shown in Figure 3-1.

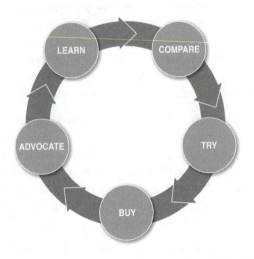

Figure 3-1   The typical buyer's journey places a premium on customers influencing other customers.

Often, sales listening provides the primary feedback loop for product and service development. If a customer needs a new feature, chances are that some other customers also need that feature. Also, a good salesperson knows from the gut which messages helped her close a deal compared to which messages did *not* resonate. It would be foolish to ignore this feedback.

When sales and marketing organizations are well connected, this feedback is a primary source for new messaging guidance, but sometimes it is given too much credence and drowns out any other form of feedback.

Except in small companies, salespeople do not talk to prospects unless they are likely to become customers—or are *already* customers. Existing customers have already somewhat bought into the central messaging structure of a brand, so this is a skewed sample for your feedback. Feedback from sales people can be helpful for understanding how to retain existing customers or close deals, but it does little to help to learn how to grow your client list. You learn how to grow your list by listening to the kind of people your salespeople do *not* interact with.

But there is an even bigger reason relying on sales feedback alone does not tell the whole story: Sales feedback is anecdotal, subject to all the errors common in expert opinions from political punditry to baseball scouting. Mainly, the biases stem from small sample sizes. When a sales rep talks to five clients and forms an opinion based on these interactions, it excludes the other thousand prospects the rep never talked to. Which pitch works (and which doesn't) is subject to all kinds of variables, including regional and industry-related differences. Sales reps are particularly susceptible to bias because they typically are assigned to a region or an industry. These differences are important for companies to learn, but companies get in trouble when they try to generalize from them.

As an example, not too many years ago, IBM made a big change in how they market blade servers—small rack-mounted computer servers that are especially easy to start up and take down. It all started when IBM salespeople in the United States noted that the idea of comparing the flexibility of blade servers to a drive-up window resonated with their clients. The company decided to make the drive-up window the centerpiece of blade server messaging. Images of cars pulling up to a drive-up service center were central to the campaign. When the campaign rolled out, IBM saw huge regional fluctuations in effectiveness. In some parts of the world, the campaign didn't work at all. In Italy, for example, they don't have drive-up windows. In other parts of the world, drive-up windows are used only for fast food, and not all the connotations associated with fast food are positive. In some regions, the negatives outweighed the positives. IBM learned from this experience that they need a more representative sample of listening data before rolling out a campaign worldwide.

Customer Support Listening

Companies should be wary of restricting their feedback loops to sales and support. Support feedback is even more susceptible than sales feedback to small sample biases. The main bias in support feedback is its focus on that swath of existing customers who are not satisfied with the product for some reason.

By all means, companies should log this feedback and fix the problems for all of their customers. But the insights are not particularly helpful for marketing. By focusing on existing customers, the feedback comes from people who

---

DANIEL KAHNEMAN, ON STATISTICAL BIASES

In his book *Thinking Fast and Slow*, Nobel Laureate Daniel Kahneman uses 40 years of research on diverse subjects to show how we make decisions. We like to think that our decisions are always rational and carefully considered. But often they are knee-jerk reactions. Understanding how and when we make these two different types of decisions affects the way we think about our own decision making.

Kahneman gives names to these two decision personas: System 1 and System 2.

System 1 is the knee-jerk response. Much of our lives are governed by this system because of the uncertainty we face and the speed with which our uncertain decisions come at us. System 1 is highly efficient for this. And most of the time, it's right. But sometimes, the very system we use to make quick decisions gets us jumping to conclusions when we don't need to, partly because it is easier and partly because we are just so sure we are right, we don't even consider that we could be wrong.

System 2 is the rational, reasonable decision maker. When we doubt our knee-jerk response, our minds engage System 2 to check and validate our decisions. This is the system that computer scientists have tried to replicate, under the belief that it is the system we primarily use to make decisions. The reality is that this system is secondary because System 2 is slow and lazy. Humans are cognitive misers. We don't want to expend the mental energy needed to engage System 2 unless we have to. When we don't have time or energy to do the math, we guestimate. System 1 is the process we use to guestimate. And it is susceptible to all kinds of biases, which are just shortcuts around using System 2.

---

have already bought into the idea of the product. This feedback says nothing about how to get more prospects bought in. Moreover, support feedback is focused on the customer experience and on the product or service itself; it's valuable, yes, but not terribly important for adjusting marketing messages.

Market Research Listening

Traditionally, when companies wanted to find out about what their clients and prospects needed, they turned to market research. Market research is traditionally performed using social science—surveys, focus groups, etc.

Humans make a lot of preventable mistakes. And if we make these mistakes over and over without thinking about them, they develop into biases. We defend ourselves, claiming that we've been doing the job for years, so we can know things without checking. But we don't know what we don't know, and we end up repeating the same mistakes over and over again. Biases are fatal to organizations, especially when they appear to be right most of the time.

For example, a 1% response rate is considered good throughout demand-generation marketing. So it is used as a standard to justify continuing to spend marketing dollars on those tactics. When we point out that a marketer can achieve between a 5% and 10% response rate with other tactics, we don't always get agreement. We can trot out case after case where a tactic we're proposing produced 10 times the response rate, and still organizations resist. Why? Because they don't want to do the math. The 1% response rate tactics are within their comfort zones. They'd rather not go outside their comfort zones to engage System 2 and consider reinvesting their dollars in better performing tactics.

A central point of this book is to convince people to jettison their biases and do the math. This means learning all the new data sources and how they help achieve better success than the already successful marketing you're doing. It means building a culture of data-driven marketing that restlessly reinvents better ways of acquiring and engaging with new audiences. Throughout this book we point out typical marketing biases and show how doing the math can generate better results.

The idea is to find a representative sample of the target clients and ask them what their biggest challenges and pain points are and then glean insights from this data for development, marketing, and sales. This kind of research is, of course, valuable and should be given more investment in an outside-in transformation. But it has limitations, the biggest being that market research methods such as surveys and focus groups can answer only the questions that you ask. Market research can't detect new trends or alert you to new issues or ideas.

An outside-in marketer might be tempted to use existing marketing research to plan content marketing, but this can also be limiting. Most companies have market research only about their products and services, not their customer's content needs. You might know a lot about which features customers love or hate about your product, but you don't necessarily know what your customers are interested in, which problems they need solved, or which subjects interest them. You might know what they want in your product, but not what they want in your content.

Competitive Analysis Listening

The other form of traditional market research is competitive analysis. Again, this is vital, but it also has limitations. If a competitor has a larger share of a particular market than you do, the reason might not stem from your company or your products. It might be about geographic preferences, long-held relationships, or countless other reasons. Determining these reasons is the essential activity of competitive analysis.

This practice is evolving with new sources of data to a point where companies can not only learn why they fail to compete in a given market but what it would take to compete. When you stack all these market opportunities against each other, you can get a good picture of where to invest in beating the competition and where to let your competitors win or whether to partner with them. The more focused you are in your investments, the better your chance at success. So prioritizing investment opportunities is an essential aspect of competitive analysis.

Embracing these new sources of data is the essential cultural shift in market research. Unless you integrate new sources of data into competitive analysis, you risk investing in unwinnable opportunities. These new sources of data—keyword research, social listening, transactional data—can help you understand how to steer your company's investments toward success. Because these new sources of data stem entirely from clients and prospects, getting market researchers to integrate these types of data into their analyses will go a long way toward building an outside-in culture.

NEW KINDS OF LISTENING

The web is not just a collection of information. It's a record of user behavior. This user behavior can tell us more about clients and prospects than any other source. You are no doubt familiar with social listening, through which companies learn what people are saying about their products and brands in social media. This is a valuable source of data on your clients and prospects, but it is by no means the only source of listening on the web. It isn't even the most important one for marketers.

The most important kind of listening is keyword research. With a simple Google AdWords account, you can learn which words and phrases are most popular among your target audiences. When users search, they indicate their interests. Using keyword research, you can mine not only the topics that interest them but the problems they are trying to solve and the questions they need to answer. When these keywords are segmented by the steps of the buyer's journey, you can build a matrix of content to serve your target audience. You can even prioritize this content based on the size of the opportunity.

But don't stop there. Use those same keywords to mine conversations through social media listening. Use sentiment analysis to find negative conversations that might indicate customer problems that you can solve with your products and services. Writing about problems that your offerings solve can be among the most powerful kinds of content marketing.

Cultural Change Must Be Approached Role by Role

New sources of customer insight should not be the exclusive purview of market research. Market research is primarily charged with providing insights into corporate strategy and messaging. To truly transform into an outside-in organization, every person with digital responsibilities in marketing and communications should be able to integrate these new data sources into their everyday jobs. Ideally, this would not be a matter of interpreting

NEW WORD OR TWO OLD WORDS?

A common branding mistake that is risky in digital marketing is to create one new word from two common words. SmartCloud®, for example, was a brand name that IBM used to market its cloud solutions. Though it is a catchy, clever name, it comes with many challenges.

For example, before the brand was launched, it was functionally meaningless. Keyword research rightly showed zero search demand for the brand. This makes sense because no one had ever used the word before, so how would Google understand what the word means well enough to build search engine results pages around a query for it?

When the brand was first launched, a search for "SmartCloud" yielded the response *"Did you mean Smart Cloud?"* with the words *Smart* and *Cloud* separated by a space. Why? Because that made sense to Google. Google uses spaces between words to parse language, as do we. Humans haven't always done this, but the invention of spaces between words changed reading forever, making it accessible to the silent masses. That was 1,200 years ago, so it is hard for us to imagine writing in Western languages without spaces. And it would be almost impossible for Google or any other intelligent system to parse Western languages without them.

So when you smash words together to form brand names, you are basically creating a nonsensical string for intelligent systems like Google—and any prospects who might otherwise be interested in what you have to sell. The only way to help intelligent systems—and your clients and prospects—find your new word is to build the page around more common words and hope Google or other intelligent systems don't penalize you for being opaque. For reasons we will explain in detail later, that is getting harder and harder to do.

Google is awash in content. So, like a hiring manager who is looking for any typo to disqualify a candidate resume, Google looks for any trick or scheme to game its algorithm, and it heavily discounts pages strategy documents written by market researchers for corporate executives. The ideal transformation would help each participant in the end-to-end marketing and communications process use outside-in data in decisions.

that run afoul of its standards. So if your page has a nonsensical brand name in the heading and all the text contains plain language that your clients and prospects use in their information journeys, this will appear like gaming the system. Is the page about the nonsensical name or the topic described in plain language? Chances are that Google will prevent you from getting the search visibility your clear prose deserves.

Keyword research is a powerful tool for understanding your audience because it reflects how your target audiences think about the products and services you are trying to market. It is an urban dictionary of language usage, representing the ebb and flow of parlance. If you build digital experiences that use this language, not only will Google give you the credit you deserve but users will find your content easier to understand. This is why Google can serve as a proxy for your audience. When you ignore this signal, you will struggle to communicate with your target audience.

Are we saying not to incorporate brand names? No! Branding is important so that people have a handle on all those great messages you send about your product. In fact, if your content really catches fire, you'll eventually teach your market the brand name. Once you do, you'll want all that great content to include your brand name so it will be found when searchers do start searching for that brand name.

So how do you incorporate brand names into your content without getting penalized? The trick is to lead with the words and phrases your target audiences use and condition the conversation toward your brands. Thus, you attract the audience to come to a brand-neutral conversation and help them understand how your brands fit into this conversation. When you lead with brand names, not only will you fail to attract the traffic, you will confuse your target audience by forcing your nomenclature on them. It is just better to attract them with their own words and then build the bridge to your branding. If you're clear, this will not involve eliminating spaces between common words.

Marketing Managers

Marketing managers determine the messaging for a campaign or an event. They write briefs and help marketers downstream develop assets in line with the briefs. In an outside-in culture, these folks start by learning how clients and prospects think. They write about the product families they want to market and then they develop messages tuned to resonate with these clients and prospects.

Contrast this with an inside-out culture, in which companies build clever campaigns that attempt to differentiate their brands from the competition. When you do this, more often than not, you start with a new way of speaking and writing about a product. So, although it might be clever, it is very difficult to get your audience to understand the messaging you create. It takes a lot of advertising over a long time to brand things in the traditional inside-out way.

Creating findable digital assets is especially difficult when you coin new words and use other clever tricks to differentiate your brands to unaware clients. The new data sources tell you which words and phrases your target audience uses to find information on the product categories that interest them. Unless you use those words in your messaging, everything that happens downstream from the messaging will be hard to find through search or social means.

When you introduce new sources of data to marketing managers, you reduce their overreliance on their two current sources of data: sales and competitive analysis. As we have seen, dependence on anecdotal evidence from sales can lead to biases in the messaging framework. Similarly, an overreliance on competitive analysis leads to focusing messaging on beating the competition rather than serving client needs. If you serve client needs better than your competition, you will beat them eventually.

Because it's a culture change, not all marketing managers will go willingly. How do you persuade marketing managers to do things in a new way? Money. More and more we see that the old methods that worked in offline marketing don't work as well as more customer attention shifts online, so marketing managers will be forced to make the culture shift to new forms of data that lead them to more persuasive forms of marketing.

Content Owners

For any content asset or web page, there is an owner—the person sponsoring or managing the content. The content on an individual page might have multiple owners, who each has a stake in the assets that the page contains. In this way, pages are hubs in which content owners with interdependent business goals collaborate to create the best experiences for the client—or at least that is the ideal state.

Whether they own pages or assets, content owners need to understand how their content does its job in customer terms. That requires an understanding of what the target audience needs, which is dependent on the newer forms of data—keyword and social research. Once a page is launched, its assets can be tested for their effectiveness and improved based on those results.

Too often in digital marketing, a content owner will decide that a certain asset or page is needed without doing this research. As a result, the content doesn't have a chance to do its job. If a page or an asset is not useful to the target audience, it only detracts from the audience's experience. It might look promising but then disappoint. Now you've wasted the precious time and attention of the audience, who might or might not trust your ability to meet their future information needs, let alone their product needs.

Another common problem is duplicate content. If two product owners both decide to publish essentially the same content for the same audience and the same state in their client journeys, the result is confusing to the audience. Which page or asset is the "official" corporate-endorsed version? This is why collaboration between content owners is essential. Outside-in thinking requires all participants to understand client needs and agree to co-create what is needed rather than compete.

How do you get content owners to change their style to outside-in marketing? Much as with marketing managers, they will be motivated by money. Proving that these new data sources lead to more client and prospect conversions will convince them. Having that conversion data at their disposal will cause content owners to pay attention.

Content Developers

Traditionally, content developers were writers who learned how to create the content audiences demand on the web. These folks are the original outside-in practitioners because they have a crying need to get their content read. Content doesn't market itself, but naïve content developers sometimes think that they must merely create compelling content, and it will do the job. Once content developers discovered that if you build it, they might not come, they started paying attention to how to write findable and usable content. This meant learning what the audience needs and developing *that*.

To assist content developers to make the cultural change to outside-in marketing, you must show them how focusing this findable and usable content will cause more readers to discover and consume their content. Content developers are less likely to be motivated by money than the previously described roles have been. But no one toils away creating content happy to have no one experience what they have produced. Using analytics showing higher consumption of well-produced content can motivate the behavior you want from your content developers.

Content developers who have learned this valuable lesson have started using the new data sources to understand the needs of clients and prospects prior to writing. But this isn't enough. If every content developer in a company used the same data, they would soon develop reams of duplicate content. Keyword data alone would lead all of them to conclude that they should develop content for the highest-value words. All content developers have access to the same data. Unless they collaborate and share their work with one another, they naturally gravitate toward building multiple versions of the same content. All that content just gums up the works. Enter content strategists, who specialize in auditing content repositories and building content plans.

Content Strategists

Pushy advertising might be mere noise to the audience, who has learned to tune it out. In contrast, interactive media by its nature cannot be easily tuned out. It either does its job or is a negative experience for the audience; it is rarely neutral. For this reason, content owners often employ content strategists to make sure they do not create duplicated or otherwise difficult content experiences for the clients and prospects they are trying to serve.

Ideally, content strategists would help owners build delightful digital experiences. But many companies need more basic intervention before they can tackle the more advanced challenge.

Content strategists give content owners the freedom to focus on the business results they are trying to drive with their content, without needing to worry about the challenges of content management. Content strategists are often the glue that binds teams together, by serving as the keepers of understanding about what assets and pages are already live, how to root out needless duplication, where the gaps are in their client information journeys, and how best to fill those gaps.

For this reason, content strategists, more than any role in content marketing, must have an outside-in perspective. Too often, we have worked with content strategists who focused too heavily on the business goal of the content, without paying enough attention to how clients and prospects would help them achieve that goal. An overly narrow focus on the business goal is an inside-out perspective of influencing customers to achieve *your* goals. You're not saying you want to help clients and prospects achieve *their* goals. But aligning with their goals comes first. Only after you understand their goals can you develop a strategy that focuses on aligning your business goal to theirs. Demonstrating the effectiveness of content conceived this way can go a long way toward convincing content strategists that the outside-in approach is their best strategy.

Mike once had an experience with a client introducing a new product that followed a tried-and-true content strategy. The client was aiming for a big splash announcement of what they hoped would be an annual conference on an emerging business area. But they were concerned because their last new conference had flopped. Mike persuaded the content strategist to "hedge their bets" by introducing a series of content marketing campaigns designed to call attention to this new business area. After months of effort, the traffic to the site was still tepid, so they decided not to hold the conference. Now, maybe this might seem like a failure, but it was a lot better than spending tons of money to hold an unsuccessful conference—and the company thanked Mike for helping them avert disaster. None of this would have been possible without paying attention to the numbers—the new data that showed that this topic just wasn't ready for prime time.

By all means, content owners need to be clear with content strategists about the business goals of the content. But that discussion needs to start with understanding how the content serves the needs of the audience because meeting the needs of the audience is required before you'll have their attention to persuade them toward your business goals.

Information Architects

Before we called them content strategists, the people who served as user advocates typically called themselves either information architects (IA) or user experience (UX) designers. Both of these roles are still vital to effective content marketing, especially in larger organizations.

Information architects structure the navigation and information flow of a site, designing the *context* for content. On the web, the context of a page or an asset is expressed in the links between it and other pages or assets. IAs play an extremely important role because people who develop content focus on the trees (individual pages, assets) under development and lose site of the forest (the collection of pages, assets). When clients and prospects come to your site, they see the forest and only make sense of the trees in the context of the forest. Having both perspectives is essential.

Information architects can fall into inside-out traps if they are not carefully managed. The main trap IAs fall into is getting caught up in corporate naming and taxonomy discussions. When the navigation links, such as the header or footer links on a website, mostly use brand names and company jargon, it confuses both users and the search engines employed to find relevant information. That's why information architects must encourage customer language in every area, from the text itself to bread crumb trails to URL names to hashtags and more.

The culture change required for IAs might be easier for them than for others because they've always been attuned to outside influences to do their jobs well. Good information architects were doing "card sorts" even in the 1990s—where they convened a group of typical website users to arrange words on cards to correspond with larger categories—as a way to organize topics into menus. Mike has worked with IAs to replace card sorts with new data sources, by mining social media and search keywords for names to test and then conducting A/B tests on live sites and comparing click-through and conversion rates.

Companies need to have taxonomy and metadata standards, but the standards should primarily focus on industry-standard terminology, and only secondarily on corporate nomenclature. Clients use brand names when they are ready to purchase, for example, but those brand names cannot be the sum total of links on a site. As we've emphasized, you must use new forms of listening, such as keyword research and social media, to learn industry-standard terminology through the new data sources.

After IAs consult these outside-in data sources, they can use their talent and training to construct architectures just as they always have—with one crucial difference: They have cast a wide net to identify the best language to use for the site's navigation rather than hoping that some qualitative techniques will uncover what they need, and using big data to do an exhaustive search of nomenclature ensures that no important term will be missed.

User Experience Designers

User experience designers are similar to information architects, but a UX designer does not just focus on the navigation flow, looking in addition at the design of a web experience (read: collection of pages) to determine what will be the easiest and most intuitive information design.

UX designers focus on testing different designs in lab settings, live sites, or both. Because they test multiple versions of the same experience and choose the one that most of the users in the test found easiest to use, UX designers are by definition outside-in practitioners.

Still, UX designers can fall into an inside-out trap if they present different designs assuming that the user found a way to the site. They often present the experience as though it is the first thing the user sees in a day and as if the user did not have an agenda ahead of time. Neither assumption reflects real life. The information users see is relevant to their information journey, which usually starts outside the site, in search or social experiences. An experience can be easy to use in a lab setting but not in a live setting because it does not flow with information journeys that begin externally.

For example, a typical information journey progresses from basic to more advanced or detailed information. If every experience begins with basic information, it doesn't apply to an audience familiar with the basics. If they have already read about that concept, they need the next logical step in their information journey. The same experience might be perfect for that journey one day and irrelevant the next.

Often, the more telling experience is how the user found a way to the site in the first place. A typical scenario begins with a user searching for a specific keyword and then clicking one of the links in the search engine results page. When she lands on your page, she scans it and jumps to the conclusion that it is either relevant or not. If she deems it irrelevant, she hits the Back button to jump back to the search results page, and perhaps refines her keyword. Only if she deems the site relevant to her search does she begin to engage. At that point, UX means a great deal, but the context of her search must not be ignored.

The search keyword is a signpost in the user's information journey. Learning users' keywords and building experiences for them is the central practice of outside-in UX design, which concentrates on the buyer's journey. You learn how well a page fits into the journey by learning which keywords and social cues help your audience find content on your site.

How do you help UX practitioners to avoid these inside-out traps? One way is to avoid total reliance on user testing for their conclusions. As helpful as in-person user tests can be in designing the experience of a site, using data collected "in the wild" from A/B testing or from user session recording software can uncover problems not seen in artificial situations in most test scenarios. Because good UX folks are externally motivated to provide the best experience, they should have an easier time making the culture shift than those in some other roles.

Web Designers

Web designers focus on the layout, typography, and color palette of pages. Whereas UX designers focus on how the information flows or how pages work, web designers focus on the look and feel of websites. Form follows function, so they need to live within the design constraints of the UX designers and IAs, but web designers can add some white space, simplify the color palette, or use more readable fonts, for example.

You might think that web design is the most inside-out of all digital marketing roles. After all, what data would web designers use to inform decisions about white space, fonts, or color schemes? Designers need to pay attention to what users scan for when they land on a page. Study after study suggests that users scan pages before determining that they are worth their time and attention. If what they are scanning for does not hit them between the eyes when they arrive on a page, they are likely to hit the Back button. Understanding what they are scanning for and giving it the appropriate emphasis (tastefully, of course) is the clearest path to success for web designers.

In our experience, designers constitute the most critical and challenging aspect of outside-in cultural transformation because designers frequently prefer graphical elegance to effectiveness. Mike often rails against the new design chic of eliminating the website search box in favor of an elegant magnifying glass icon—forcing would-be searchers to click the icon before they can even enter their search keyword. Analytics show a dramatic drop in search activity with this design, probably due to users not noticing where the search box is.

Even worse, this bias toward graphics causes designers to want to minimize the text on a page. That's all well and good for push media, where you have a captive audience, but in digital pull media, text is how search engines find pages and how users judge them for relevance at first glance. Aside from infographics, heavy graphical treatments don't communicate relevance very well. In the absence of sufficient textual cues, users tend to bounce rather than engage.

Many of the designers we have worked with have shown an understandable frustration with search marketing because search engines struggle to understand graphics. Web designers feel forced to increase the size of the copy hole to accommodate search optimization, which is considered bad visual design. Unfortunately, text is the primary cue to help users (and the search engines that mimic them) determine the relevance of results to their search keywords. Skimping on text for the sake of design elegance is the most common way digital development teams undercut their own success.

How do you convince designers to put aside their bias against "gray pages" of text? Focus on results. Designs are only as good as the results they generate. Force UX designers to go back to basics: If it is a good design for people, it must test well. Don't allow designers to take the snobbish view that the masses have poor taste. If they want to cash a check from the marketing department, they must be willing to sell stuff. Is it a hard sell for you? Yes, but designers are too important to marketing for you to let them live in an inside-out world.

How do you sell it to them? Appeal to their interest in producing something that does the job. In one situation, we tested several designs to determine which one had the lowest bounce rate for a critical page. Most of the designs were the typical "pretty" approach, where what was seen "above the fold" on a typical laptop screen was merely a nice image. One design shrunk the image to reveal several lines of text. That text-heavy design yielded a 20% bounce rate, while the image-heavy designs had 90% bounce rates. Everything else about the pages was the same, so presenting this kind of evidence to your designers can be very compelling. Designers need to be retaught in some cases that good design is about what users want, not what looks pretty.

Web Developers

Web developers code pages according to the design and content specs they receive from the team. They also commonly test pages on development servers before turning them on for use by everyone who has a browser and an Internet connection. It's no exaggeration to say that one false move by a web developer can prevent the success of an entire team. For example, if the developer doesn't code the robots.txt metadata correctly, the site will not be indexed by search engines and will never be found by clients or prospects.

Web developers are subject to other inside-out traps that they would best avoid by using the new sources of data. Title tags, URLs, headings, links, alt attributes, and countless small details can make the difference between a page ranking on the first page in search results or the fourth. If it's not on the first page, it will not get many visitors, no matter how high the quality. Search engines are improving, but they still rely heavily on how pages are coded for ranking. And most of the negative ranking factors come from the code. Appearing to spam the metadata, for example, is a sure way to get your page off the first page in Google.

Even though web developers are traditionally attuned to the new sources of data, it's worth making sure they buy into the culture. They can fall into

AN APPLICATION OF THINKING FAST AND SLOW: THE PSYCHOLOGY OF DIGITAL

Daniel Kahneman's work on organizational change has practical applications to digital marketing. Indeed, his framework can be used to approximate how users consume websites. Consider this scenario:

Lizzy is a highly educated millennial who works as an editor in the publishing field. She searches for "structured mark-up" in Google and gets a ton of results. She scans the first search engine results page and clicks the most likely link without really reading the results. When she lands on the page, she scans it to determine if it is worth the effort. She decides that it is and begins reading the long-form content on the page.

What does Lizzy's mental state look like? Well, she used both System 1 and System 2 in the process of her information journey. System 1 is the primary mechanism of her scanning and clicking behavior. Scanning search results and clicking is as familiar to Lizzy as using a turn signal while driving. She doesn't need to think about it. System 2 is what she uses to read and digest the content.

A whole UX discipline has grown out of Steve Krug's imperative *Don't Make Me Think*. If you make Lizzy think when she lands on your page, you force her to engage System 2, which is slow and lazy. Not only is Lizzy in a hurry, she really doesn't want to waste mental energy either. If you force her to think, she will jump to the conclusion that your inside-out traps. A common one is fixating on building whiz-bang experiences in JavaScript or other languages, which are not fully accessible to search engines, although Google does better with that sort of thing than do the other search engines. No matter how high quality the content is, if it's not open to search crawlers, it will never even get indexed by search engines. In that case, the clever code is lost to all but the internal team that reviews it.

Web developers usually don't need to be persuaded to change their culture—they are usually surprisingly oriented to the needs of the user—but they often need exposure to data that shatters their preconceived notions of exactly what the user needs. We've frequently shown web developers before and after tests using analytics data or A/B tests of alternatives to help them see what users actually prefer. Typically, providing more facts to web developers brings them around.

---

page is not relevant before even engaging System 2, and she'll bounce back to the search engine to try another result.

When Lizzy does find your page relevant, she is ready to engage System 2. This means providing enough data, case studies, and other stuff to help her complete her information task. Once she engages System 2, she does not want to have to go back to the search results page again. Ideally, she can get everything she needs on your site. Once she engages System 2, long-form content is what she needs.

For the longest time, we have had a raging debate in our field about whether users read on the web. All kinds of studies have shown that users don't read on the web but merely scan. Our experience shows that if you get the Lizzy use case right, users do read on the web. They'll even download a longish white paper and read it on the web if it is relevant and compelling. But if you don't get the Lizzy use case right, they bounce off your page before reading, regardless of how close the content is to the query.

As pages improve and the body of evidence approaches critical mass, similar studies have come to different conclusions. Thanks to Kahneman, we now have a framework for understanding these studies. The inflection point between scanning and reading seems to be a System 1 process that determines whether a page is worth a user' time and attention.

Metrics Analysts

Metrics analysts typically analyze the effectiveness of websites in terms of visits, visitors, engagement rates, conversion rates, and other measures. These data sets are critical in understanding how effective websites can be after the content is launched.

Ideally, the content owner will have an idea of how well the site should perform, given the data about keywords and social signals. But the reality is, these data sets provide only a good starting place for how well a page or an asset will work. The real test is in how well it intercepts clients and prospects in their information journeys to help them complete their tasks. A good metrics analyst measures how well content leads to user task completion.

It might seem odd to think that a metrics analyst could fall into an inside-out trap, considering that his whole job is about gathering data on how clients and prospects use a website. But it happens. The main trap is making assumptions about traffic sources and thereby misinterpreting the data.

For example, if an analyst discovers that one-third of the visitors came from your company's home page, she might assume it was through navigation, when in reality it was probably through your internal search function. If the reports are presented without checking this fact, it might appear that users navigate more than they search on your site. In the sites for which we consult, search behavior dwarfs navigation by a large margin. Assuming that it is navigation might lead to a missed opportunity to find out which words and phrases clients and prospects use when they search inside your site. A metrics analyst who does not take advantage of this data source has fallen into an inside-out trap, with more effort placed on naming navigation items according to corporate jargon than on improving internal search and the experiences it points to.

Data doesn't analyze itself. Smart people must glean the insights needed to make excellent client experiences. This requires an outside-in perspective at the core. Like web developers, metrics analysts are very...well...analytical. More data, more facts, more information is extremely persuasive. Help an analyst understand what the data really means, and you will bring her around.

Community Managers

Otherwise known as social business managers, community managers are part media relations, part content strategist, and part content curator. They are primarily responsible for building and maintaining branded social spaces in the major social channels. In some organizations, community managers are actually the content marketers who work with content strategists and content developers to promote content through social channels.

Community managers naturally have an outside-in focus because a central part of their role is social listening. The best community managers listen for client needs in the social channels and help content strategists and developers build the needed content. They also monitor influencers and help internal content producers and bloggers connect with external influencers.

Unfortunately, while community managers have a fundamentally outside-in role, they can fall into an inside-out trap. All the listening programs on the market begin with the community manager entering some keywords and letting the tool loose to crawl the social channels for mentions of these words. Community managers then analyze the context of these mentions to determine things like the sentiment of the mention (Was it in the context of a negative review?) and the semantics of the mention (Which related words were often found in the vicinity of the mention?). These are some of the most valuable data sets a company can get. They are vital to an outside-in culture and get more attention later in the book.

The trap for community managers is entering inside-out words into the tools in the first place. If a community manager does this, the results will be skewed toward those conversations between clients who already understand the branding and jargon inherent in a company. They will not find the hidden conversations that are really about the market for your products or services but are disguised in industry-standard language. If community managers enter industry-standard keywords into the social tools, they see the whole conversation, not just the one related to a brand. What's more, monitoring social conversation allows you to notice the slow evolution of words that you need to target for your content.

Another inside-out trap for community managers is featuring executives and other brand stewards as the primary thought leaders of the company rather than featuring the experts or developers. Because executives often have near-term revenue goals to achieve, the messages they create in social settings will tend toward the kind of thing you might read in a press release rather than the kind of thing social media users want to like and share. A true outside-in community manager will find the experts who have external credibility and promote their writing. Experts wouldn't have external credibility if they constantly acted like shills for their companies.

Fortunately, these inside-out traps are easily rectified because few community managers are in love with their own ideas. Their natural disposition to listen to their community allows you to show them the light quite easily.

Barriers to the Outside-In Culture Change

If, by now, you are persuaded that culture change is essential to transform your marketing to outside-in marketing, you might be wondering what can get in the way of that culture change. Next we talk about the five most common barriers. Luckily, just being aware of these barriers can be enough to overcome them. It's when they sneak up on you that they are most dangerous.

Barrier 1: Brand Building Is Valued More Than Customer Building

One of the objections we often hear from brand marketers is that outside-in marketing is just a more sophisticated demand-generation engine but that it can't help a company *build* brands. Think of how iconic brands such as Apple, Coca-Cola, or some of the P&G brands were built: Their companies created a visual language and told stories promoting the brand with that language. When we talk to brand managers, the idea of using primarily text-based media to build a visual language falls flat. It lacks the production values and the stunning visuals needed to raise awareness and brand lift.

Some of this criticism of outside-in marketing is warranted. You can't paint a brand image with a search ad or a tweet. The simplifying principles on which the web was built (limited colors, fonts, and load times) make using the web alone for brand building an iffy proposition. But that's changing. As the web becomes more and more visual with the rise of Pinterest, YouTube, and the addition of photos to just about everything, brand marketers have all the tools of brand building available online that they have always had offline. Regardless, building brands must take second place to actual sales when the two conflict.

In addition, the web is a transactional medium. People are self-directed in their information discovery. They want to complete tasks. Aside from YouTube videos, the information on the web is rarely passively consumed. The kind of brand management that led to Coke becoming one of the most valuable brands on the planet requires a degree of passivity. That's why Coke still has a very large TV ad budget. An audience that just wants to lean back and let images wash over them is easier to influence. Coke also does a lot of outdoor advertising, focusing on putting its brand language in front of captive audiences.

Of course, there is still room for offline media for brand building. And perhaps it will continue to be the primary way brands are built. But that doesn't mean outside-in marketing has no value in building brand awareness—especially in telling the stories that help audiences identify with brand language, online and offline.

The primary value of digital marketing for brand lift is in audience targeting. For example, consider a YouTube campaign that serves multiple versions of the same clever ad and measures the results. YouTube has analytics built in that measure video abandonment. If you have a well-designed YouTube channel, you can quickly test multiple versions of the ads to see which ones tend to be watched all the way through versus those that users click away from partway through.

Where does big data come into this? You can measure all kinds of things about videos that will help you get a sense of how effective they are to the target audience, including how often they are shared and by whom, how well they are reviewed, and what is the text analytics of the comments. Of course, you also have a plethora of search metrics to analyze. All these data sets can be fed back into your campaign, and you can then buy the most appropriate air time and use the most effective ads within those buys.

Outside-in marketing is not merely a mechanism for learning more about the audience to build your brand. It is also a way to tell stories. For example, more and more all the time, audiences are using their tablets while they watch TV. With an integrated approach to TV and online media, you can build hooks in the ads that encourage the audience to continue the story online. Perhaps your TV ad tells just the first bit of a story, but the other parts unfold on your YouTube channel.

More than anything else, the culture of avoiding digital media for brand building is hurting brands rather than helping them. Think of how so-called millennials, who grew up with the Internet, view a brand that is noticeably absent in critical conversations. One of James' current jobs involves helping the IBM Cloud Computing digital team build a more outside-in website. Besides search optimization, one of the first things he did was look at Wikipedia to see how the IBM brand was represented in the Cloud Computing topic. To his horror, it was nonexistent. So he edited the topic to include IBM as a provider of cloud-based solutions and built a new topic to describe what these solutions were and how they were branded.

Brand managers might be nonplussed by efforts to shore up a Wikipedia page, which is almost entirely encyclopedic text. But our data suggested that the absence of IBM—the company that invented computing as a service (aka cloud)—was creating confusion in a large audience that depends on Wikipedia for answers to more basic questions. The overwhelming attitude among those surveyed was that IBM didn't have cloud solutions because they were not listed on that page. For this audience, one of the best things IBM could do was to make sure they were present on Wikipedia. And we can tell similar stories for IBM's presence on the first page of search engines for the words and phrases the target audiences use to find the information they need.

Somehow companies need to transform the culture of devaluing digital content for brand building. It certainly can't be the only tactic a brand manager uses. But if you ignore it, you will fail, especially in the age of the hyper-digital audience.

Barrier 2: Marketing Is Stuck in Advertising

To be effective, outside-in marketing must shake the stereotype of advertising, which requires the marketing organization to act more like an editorial department and less like an advertising department.

For example, one of the first things James did when he was editor in chief of ibm.com was to change the style guide from something an ad copy writer might endorse to something an editor would love. One of the key changes was a simple word replacement. He replaced the word *copy* in the style guide with *content*. Why? Well, *copy* has a connotation of ad copy, and he wanted the IBM writers to think about their creations in more sophisticated terms than an advertising copywriter uses. James wanted them to think and write like journalists because he knew that it is more effective to the self-directed audience than when they think like advertisers.

After he published the style guide, a communications manager teased James by asking why he built something for a role that did not exist. "Don't you know that marketers are *not* writers. They just hire agencies to write their copy? If you want something written internally, talk to communications," he said. It never occurred to James that the communications manager was right until after he had built the style guide. Just about every department in IBM lauded him for the accomplishment, except marketing, in part because it challenged them to grow beyond their comfort zones. Ultimately, it worked out because marketing soon started hiring in-house writers to craft the articles traditionally written either in the communications department or in an agency. But the legacy of advertising is hard to shake.

Barrier 3: Marketing Must Be Separated from Public Relations

Once the roles within digital marketing demonstrate the outside-in principles in their work, public relations (or communications) needs its own transformation to work with marketing. In content marketing, there is no need for a wall between editorial and advertising; when you are telling true stories about how your products or services help your clients achieve success, it is not advertising. In a true outside-in organization, communications and marketing content producers work side by side to create content and promote their creations.

There is no greater need for this level of collaboration than in social settings. A sound content marketing strategy involves training experts within your company to write blog posts or microblogs to help the audience understand how your experts help clients. It puts a human face on your company and provides ready stories for your target audience.

The management of this content often happens in communications, but more and more of this work is happening in marketing organizations, which communications people need to support. Getting these two traditionally siloed organizations to work together is a critical cultural transformation, and without it, content marketing will struggle.

Barrier 4: Marketing Is Beneath Us

Another common cultural barrier to outside-in marketing involves the communications organization. Communications professionals are essential to content marketing because they are central to promoting the content a company creates. But our experience suggests that they resist doing this work because it just feels *dirty.*

To the best of our knowledge, this is a remnant of the culture of journalism, from which most communications professionals stem. In journalism, the overarching ethos is the purity of the story. News organizations, for example, often talk about a wall between editorial and advertising. It is a cardinal sin to allow the content of a story to be influenced by an advertiser, so editorial departments are kept separate from the advertising departments.

Something like this division exists at many companies, where marketing is the analogue of the advertising and communications is the analogue of editorial. In this setting, working with marketing just doesn't feel right, and communications people resist. Because content marketing demands collaboration between marketing and communications, it either breaks down this barrier or fails. If your communications department acts like they need a bath after their meeting with marketing, you must force them to work together, or your marketing will suffer.

Barrier 5: Executives Prefer Their Opinions to Data

In some organizations, this is the biggest barrier of them all. Too often, executives are accustomed to being the smartest people in the room. They have the most experience, the most strategic view, and the most information. Often, they truly are the smartest people in the room. In our experience, executives often have excellent judgment, too.

The problem, however, is that big data is smarter than all of the people in the room, including the executives. Nowhere is that more true than when it comes to content marketing.

In our experience, some executives tend to be the most concerned about the look and feel of assets. They will edit every piece of copy and will require eleventh-hour changes, all in the pursuit of perfection. In short, they will trust their gut rather than the data. They want everything they pay for to be perfect the first time. And that is the main cultural barrier to outside-in marketing. Executives need to trust the data to help them drive results faster. If they do not, the practitioners who work for them will be torn between working for results and working for perfectionistic executives.

In order to develop an outside-in culture, you have to have executive emphasis on data-driven marketing. That is step 1. Executives who buy into this concept can foster the cultural change needed.

But how do you get your executives forget their golden guts and rely on the data?

- *Instruct them.* Many executives do not realize how much data is out there and what can be done with it. They've grown accustomed to marketing being a land of opinion, so why shouldn't they trust their own? Bring in an outside speaker to teach the C-suite that the world has changed. Leave them articles from the *Harvard Business Review*. Give them this book! Don't assume that they know how the world has changed. Expose them to the change, and you might be pleasantly surprised at how they adapt.

- *Tell them.* Most people need stories to help them change their approach. When you provide more information, you make people more learned, but when you tell a story, you move them to act. Tell them a story about how we listened to the data and it worked. Give them a case study that illuminates best practices. Make sure that you communicate in terms of money whenever possible because they might just let increased sales trump their opinion.

- *Show them.* For some executives, there is nothing more persuasive than letting them know that their competitors are beating them to the punch. If you can show how competitors are already using big data in their content marketing, few executives will not rise to that bait. Just make sure that you have your facts straight because if your competitors aren't doing it yet, that is *not* a fact you want to call attention to.

- *Challenge them.* If all else fails, you can follow their instructions to the letter, as you usually do, but with one twist: Conduct an A/B test with their version and with another version. If they win, let it go. But if they lose, challenge them with the results. It won't be a comfortable meeting, but very few executives relish the prospect of you testing everything they tell you to do. Usually this tactic ends the meddling in short order.

Executives generally are rather smart—that's how they got the job. Don't be too intimidated to show them the better way. You're not wrong about this one, and they need to get the message. If they are as smart as they think they are, they will realize that we don't want to act on anyone's opinion—except our customers'.

The approach we lay out for collecting customer opinion at scale leads to better results than any single opinion, no matter how experienced and smart it might be. Those smart opinions are just the first thing to test and not the last word on what to do. When you start consistently doing what your customers want, it's amazing how quickly you'll start to look like a genius.

Wrapping Up: How Culture Eats Process

Speaking of process, we've found that too many marketers, especially in big companies, have blind faith in their process and fail to recognize how their company's culture eats their well-intended processes for lunch every day.

You can design the tools and processes to enable excellent content marketing. But ultimately, the work is done by people. People will not buy into your processes or use your tools and education unless they are convinced that it's the best way to be effective.

Every role within marketing and communications needs to embrace the culture of focusing on objective results rather than their own subjective perspectives of what quality assets look like or behave like. Too often, we see "specialist disease," where individual practitioners carry the best practices of their role to extreme conclusions without considering the necessary trade-offs that actually result in increased sales. No single one of these special roles can, by itself, carry the day. Marketing is the interplay of all of these roles, with the overarching goal of increasing the number of customers and the amount they spend. While companies can strive to create processes that optimize decision making for increased revenue, they must also recognize the culture that has allowed specialist disease to suboptimize these processes, by making the text a writer's decision, the look and feel a designer's decision, the targeting a marketing manager's decision...with each of these decisions driven by pure instinct in some cases, rather than by data, and with an executive looming overhead who can veto anything that doesn't pass muster in his or her mind.

You might have observed that culture is a topic hardly ever discussed inside your company. In a sense, it's like asking a fish, "How's the water?" only to get the response, "What water?" Culture is an unseen, unspoken force, which is part of what gives it power. Culture causes us to go along with things that we might otherwise question—things that don't stand up to cold, hard facts. For that reason, you must confront any aspect of your corporate culture that gets in the way of getting closer to your customer, satisfying your customer, and doing it more and more rapidly.

When culture stops you from using big data to drive your content marketing, it's the culture that needs to change. Consciously approaching culture as a living changeable entity is the first step to shifting organizational behaviors to adapt to the reality of big data.

In this chapter, we've examined the need for transforming culture to enable outside-in marketing. But that isn't the only problem facing companies in their transition to this new approach. Companies face the daunting prospect of transforming their marketing infrastructures. Building the tools and technologies to help marketers do outside-in marketing is no small challenge. Getting the data analysis to the right people in the right time frame to help them collaborate and make better and faster decisions involves all the challenges of big data. This deserves a chapter all its own, and that's exactly what we talk about in Chapter 4.

BILL HUNT, ON USING SEARCH KEYWORD MINING TO TRANSFORM YOUR MARKETING

Bill Hunt is the president of Back Azimuth Consulting, which focuses on helping companies understand the voice of their customer by aggregating multiple digital signals into actionable insights, product innovation, and messaging strategies.

How do you help clients to think about their campaigns from a customer (outside-in) perspective rather than from an internal (inside-out) approach?

We start with telling them to listen to the "voice of the consumer" and demonstrate through the volume of searches for related keywords and mining social media conversations what their customers are asking for. It is often a big surprise to the client what people are actually interested in vs. what they are presenting to them. We have developed a process called The Searcher Continuum, which uses query data to show them the volume of interest from the beginning of the search process through customers using the product or service.

How do you help clients adopt more of an outside-in culture?

In the majority of the cases, after seeing the data and process described above, companies have the epiphany that they need to change from a unidirectional to a bidirectional approach. It is still a huge challenge to get them to adopt something new, especially when they feel they are losing control of the message. That seems to be the scariest element of the outside-in approach, as brands have told consumers what they need to know. We try to make them understand that they are still in control of the message, but now they are doing it in a way that is more relevant to consumers. While we have not been successful getting companies to completely change, we do have a great track record of changing the thinking, especially in lead and demand generation, which is a start.

Do you find that different roles within the company require different approaches to help them?

This was one of the biggest learnings I have had over the years. Every project starts with us trying to understand the roles and agendas of each of the roles. Presenting the opportunity and changes necessary based on roles makes it more actionable and "safe" to each person. Trying to explain algorithms and data mining to marketers often results in a deer-in-headlights reaction, but showing them outcomes and actions moves the process along. For budget owners and finance folks, showing potential savings and incremental revenue appeals to them. Many companies are still focused on clicks or exposure and assume that conversions will follow.

Another big challenge with both senior and junior members is the additional work we need them to do. In many cases, they wrote a check to an agency team and then saw the final commercial or deliverables not knowing what goes into it. An outside-in approach requires a level of effort from internal teams that was not necessary before, and explaining the effort vs. reward to these levels is critical to success.

Which approaches to search keyword discovery and selection do clients typically overlook?

They overlook the simple things, like looking at what they are actually saying in the keyword. Most companies, no matter what the keyword used, try to sell them. However, they need to look at the variations and ask the question "Why did they enter this keyword, and what do we need to present to match the interest?"

How do you see big data affecting what you do for clients?

Big data has made it easier for people to understand the value of data from mashing up various data sources they never have before. Some get it and run with it, while others seem to become scared by it because it often showcases a poor strategy or a misunderstanding of their target markets. Overall, I think as businesses accept and make data-driven marketing a strategic activity, it will make my services and approaches more valuable to them.

What do you see as the biggest challenge that clients need to be ready for?

The biggest challenge is the effort in mining the data. We can do a certain level of automated mining and filtering, but it requires human effort to make decisions and understand the intent of the consumer, and we find the client is not prepared to do this. They often try to pass it off to the agency, but they do not have the knowledge of the company and products, and their multiperson "team structure" makes this work cost-prohibitive.

4

Infrastructure Transformation: Targeted Content

It was one of those moments when each member of the team started turning from side to side to see what each other team member thought—almost as though a tennis match had broken out right in front of them.

Apparently it was a difficult question: "Why are IT people, rather than marketers, responsible for your website search engine?"

You probably know what website search is: It's the little box in the upper-right corner of your site where your visitors type in words that they think will help them find pages on your site. This client had just finished explaining that the reason that their website search was awful is that it was owned by the IT team. So, the obvious next question was "Why?"

And, honestly, no one knew. Or at least no one would say. But the real answer is that no one wanted to admit that they were afraid of the technology—that marketers so utterly lacked confidence in dealing with technology that they would rather cede ownership of this critical means of satisfying customers than take the risk of appearing dumb.

We're hoping for more from you, dear reader. In fact, it is essential for you to be willing to seem as ignorant as they come. Because technology changes so fast that no one stays on top of all of it for very long. You need to be willing to ask the dumb questions, probe for the right answers, and make the right decisions based on what you're told.

And that's what this chapter is about. Are you ready to engage—really dive into the deep end—on the technology decisions that each year become more critical to your marketing success?

See, you've started the process of helping the various roles within your marketing organization embrace the culture of data-driven decisions. This is crucial if you want to transform your organization toward data-driven content marketing. But it obviously is not enough. In parallel, you will need to start building intelligent content systems. These systems combine data from external sources, such as Google AdWords, and internal sources, such as your web performance analytics systems, to develop role-specific insights for your marketing organizations.

For those readers who skipped ahead, when we talk about data-driven content marketing, we mean *inbound* marketing. Inbound marketing is the method of attracting audiences to your website to engage in your content experiences. If you do a good job with inbound marketing, some of the audience members who engage with your content will become clients of your business. There are other types of data-driven content marketing. *Outbound* marketing, for example, uses content to engage audiences on experiences outside your website, such as social platforms or third-party syndicators. These can be effective, but in our experience, inbound marketing is the most effective type of content marketing.

The needed marketing technology for inbound marketing transformation can be quite complex and well outside your comfort zone. We don't want to oversimplify the problem nor give you a false sense of security. This is hard work. But the problem is easier than many of our clients seem to think, at least when they first start grappling with it. The key is to think of the platform as serving audiences—in this case, all the folks involved in planning, writing, building, and publishing content experiences for their external audiences. When you put people in the middle of the process, the technology becomes merely a set of tools to serve them. Serving people is what marketers excel at.

In this chapter, we lay out an end-to-end system of content marketing technology that contains three key types of components:

- *Audience research systems.* These technologies allow research on the target audience and the markets they occupy. There are many ways to analyze your audience, but the two most important are keyword research tools and social media listening tools. These systems help you gauge the size of your opportunity.

- *Content messaging systems.* Some of the most widely used systems are used for creating and controlling the actual content itself, such as video editors and content management systems. But other technologies, such as for managing taxonomies, might be equally important. These systems help you execute on your opportunity.

- *Audience feedback systems.* These technologies, such as web analytics and social analytics tools, analyze information about the performance of live content on and off your website to help your marketers improve it over time. These systems keep score of how well you have taken advantage of your opportunity.

There are many ways to look at the interlocking technologies that comprise a working content marketing system, but the main point is not how you divide them up but how you get yours to work at maximum effectiveness. Most companies have at least some pieces of all three types of systems, but the place for you to start your improvement might depend on your level of maturity in your infrastructure transformation.

For example, if you are just starting to build content from an outside-in strategy, you should focus your efforts on audience research systems. But if you already have a healthy set of content, it makes more sense to start by auditing what you already have, using your audience feedback systems and using audience research systems to discover new opportunities to fill gaps.

We realize that you might approach this chapter with trepidation; marketers are not always known for their technical skills. Don't worry. Content marketing certainly requires its share of digital savvy, but you don't need to become an IT person to succeed at content marketing.

Let the techies figure out the APIs and databases and the rest of the gorpy details. Think of your role as being the same as for the electrical system in your house. You don't need to know where all those wires go behind your walls. You don't need to be a trained electrician. You just need to know where people can plug stuff in. You should learn the data needs of your content marketing so that you can give your software developers the requirements they need to wire your marketing house properly.

The first system to wire up is your audience research.

Audience Research Systems

This book is called *Outside-In Marketing* because it is based on the central premise that if you build the content your audience is looking for—primarily using search engines—you will have a much better chance to achieve your marketing business results than if you build the content you want published and push it on unwilling audiences.

Of course, you don't simply give the content away for free—not all of it, anyway. You give much of it away, and you require your audience to register for some of it—when they're ready. These registrations become leads in your sales pipeline. A portion of these leads become revenue. In a nutshell, that's the business value of inbound content marketing. In some cases, the content could lead to direct sales.

To achieve these happy outcomes, you must know what content your audience wants. Regardless of subject area, your audience wants content that satisfies a need—in most cases, content that alleviates pain points. How do you identify their pain points? The easiest techniques are to use search keyword research and social media listening. We'll tee up keyword research first.

Search Keyword Research

If finding out what your target audience searches for is job one, and keyword research is a top method, what do you use to do it? Keyword research tools, of course.

The simplest free keyword research tool to use, and the one to start with if you've had no experience, is Google Trends. Google Trends is less powerful than other keyword tools, but it truly excels in one area: visually comparing the changing demand for two or more related keyword phrases, which can help you decide which phrase is the one your customers tend to use, as shown in Figure 4-1.

For most marketers, Google Trends isn't enough. They need tools that can show actual search volume numbers—how many searches were done each month for that keyword. Luckily, just about every search engine has such a tool that's available for free to anyone who signs up for a paid search account. (You don't have to be actually running a campaign or spend any money, but you do have to have an account.)

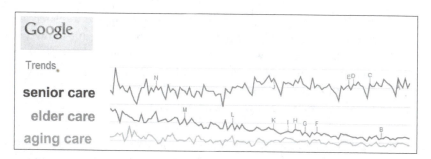

Figure 4-1 A Google Trends report showing related keyword phrases.

The most-used of these free keyword research tools is Google Keyword Planner. Because the numbers of searches for paid and organic searches are the same, Google Keyword Planner turns out to be a pretty good tool for understanding audience intent in general. Google counts the number of searches it finds that contain the keywords every month, and Google Keyword Planner helps you discover similar keywords as related searches.

When you enter a word or phrase related to your marketing campaign into Google Keyword Planner, it returns about 100 related keywords, along with the monthly search volume for each keyword. It uses semantics and search behavior to determine the most relevant keywords. Often the keywords it returns are far more popular than the keyword you put in, so the tool provides insights into how your target audience describes things differently than you do inside your company.

As helpful as Google Keyword Planner is, it does have some limitations that lead content marketers to use other (paid) tools:

- *It shows keyword volumes only for Google.* While this might be fine in a country such as Sweden, where nearly 100% of searches are made on Google, in the United States, Bing handles a significant number of searches, and in China and Russia, the main search engines are Baidu and Yandex, respectively. So you might need other sources of volume data in some countries.

- *Its suggestions are based on your paid search campaign.* Rather than showing all related searches to the keywords you enter, Google tries to show words related to those you have entered already. You can improve the results by entering a lot more words, but doing so is laborious.

- *It often shows false positives.* Just because Google suggests a related keyword doesn't mean that it's right for you. Google doesn't know your business; it just shows words that seem to be related to the keyword entered, but words are ambiguous and might not mean to you what they mean to another business. As one check, you might want to focus on keywords you've seen your competitors use.

The best keyword research combines a variety of keyword data sources to return more accurate results than Google Keyword Planner can return by itself. Think of keyword research as a series of Venn diagrams. Each phrase you enter returns a set of results. When you overlay multiple such related phrases, you find the most relevant subset of words that also have enough demand to make them worth your while, as shown in Figure 4-2.

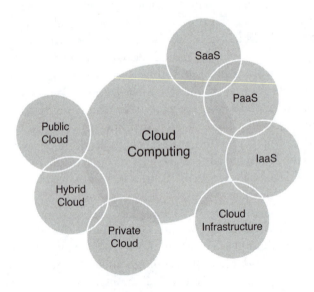

Figure 4-2   The beginnings of a keyword research project.

Your search marketers might have their own systems for building keyword lists combining the major data sources, and this might be perfectly fine in a small company. But if you have more than 1,000 search landing pages, you need a system that governs keyword usage across multiple campaigns and brands to ensure that you don't duplicate efforts and compete against yourself for your audience's limited attention. A paid keyword research tool shows everyone in your company the collective keyword research that your company has done.

Keyword research tools try to automatically detect those overlaps in the keyword Venn diagrams, which cuts labor and also weeds out many false positives. Though it is not the only source of audience data, your keyword research tool will provide most of the audience analysis you need.

Social Media Listening

Besides keyword research, the most important way to learn your audience is to perform social media listening. This helps you determine what conversations your target audience personas are participating in. If you learn their interests and pain points in this way, you can build engaging content for them.

Studies suggest that around 70% of the buyer journey happens prior to filling out a contact form, downloading a free trial, or in some way indicating direct interest in a product. Some of that discovery happens in venues outside your website—in forums, blogs, or other social media platforms such as Twitter. Listening to these conversations is obviously very important in learning your audience.

But how do you find the conversations of interest to your target audiences? Once again, you need tools. Most listening tools work in roughly the same way. You input the keywords related to your marketing campaigns, and the tools find conversations containing those keywords. Some tools also offer a relevance feedback loop so you can say which conversations are on point—and which are irrelevant—so that the tools can better isolate the right conversation.

Most tools can also analyze those relevant conversations for positive or negative sentiment. You can imagine that the negative sentiment conversations might be good candidates for identifying the language around pain points. Determining which negative topics have significant conversation volume can provide fodder for your content marketing.

A common mistake is to enter your brand names into the social media listening tool. While this might help you understand the social sentiment related to your brand, it cannot help you understand the conversation volume related to the problems your products are designed to solve. Most of the conversations in social media do not mention brands. They talk about issues or problems. It's your job to build and market solutions to those problems. So learning what unbranded conversations are taking place related to your solutions will get you the fullest understanding of customer pain points.

The good news is that you already know the words you need to enter into your social listening tools because you found them through your keyword research. In this way, you can understand not only the words that become the building blocks of your content but the pain points your content is designed to solve.

Your content marketing also benefits from social media listening by learning which conversations you should engage in. Think of social media content strategy as a cocktail party with many people that you don't know very well. After you get your drink, you linger on the edge of a conversation until it is appropriate to contribute. And you make sure you contribute something positive without being too pushy.

If you do it well, you might come away with a fledgling relationship with one of the participants in the conversation. At minimum, you learn a little more about what they care about.

Social content done with a self-promotional attitude resembles pushy, self-congratulatory content marketing—*inside-out* "look at me" marketing, rather than marketing intended to truly help your customers—and it does more harm than good. It is better to refrain from participating in social content than to do it badly. That said, it's not enough to simply contribute something helpful and then disappear. Developing a relationship is a commitment to being persistently helpful.

Before leaving the subject of social media, you should realize that marketers often won't use the insights from keyword research and social listening if you force them to leave their content authoring systems to check a resource on the company's intranet. Marketers are very busy and typically work on tight deadlines. Perhaps one in four marketers will be diligent enough to check a corporate resource on such things as style, let alone audience research data. Marketers need the insights integrated into the tools they use to plan, create, curate, and manage content.

So it's not only important to have the right audience research systems in place but to ensure that their insights are readily available and served up inside the content messaging systems—right when authors need them. And those very systems are our next topic.

Content Messaging Systems

Without content messaging systems, you'd have no content at all. Let's look at three main systems that produce the content in our world:

- *Content authoring systems.* These are tools to help your writers, designers, and user experience (UX) practitioners build effective web and social content. For authors and editors, the state of the art looks like a word processor but actually builds structured web content under the covers. Designers then flow this code into elegant user experiences with the help of UX experts.

- *Content management systems.* These are typically complex databases that populate web templates with content elements (headings, body copy, metatags, etc.). We say they are complex because they contain many subsystems for specific aspects of content creation and maintenance.

- *Taxonomy and tagging systems.* These databases of controlled values map the way you name products and services with the way your clients and prospects think and talk about them.

These are probably the systems you know best, but don't worry if they are not familiar to you. The following sections walk you through what you need to know.

Content Authoring Systems

Of all the systems we describe in this chapter, perhaps the most misunderstood are content authoring systems. More money has probably been spent on systems to create web pages and multimedia assets than on any other systems, and in many ways that money has been misspent.

The problem is that we have been using the wrong kinds of systems, in large measure, to create assets that do not have the characteristics needed for modern content marketing. Many content assets created today (such as white papers, case studies, and data sheets) are published in print-oriented systems such as PDF, which falls short of what is needed for today's marketing.

Modern content marketing needs well-structured content. What do we mean by that? Read on for the main requirements that are emerging for modern content, which content authoring systems are being pressed to support.

Better Findability

Simply put, if no one finds your content, it's worthless, regardless of how much effort and money went into creating it. James was the editor of a large organization within IBM that created a lot of white papers. One year, he edited 300 30- to 40-page white papers, line by line, to ensure that they were the highest quality IBM could muster. At the end of the year, the entire corpus totaled 25 downloads. So the first thing he did to start the next year was to optimize them for search (which turns out to be a simple thing for PDFs). That year, the same set of white papers got 150,000 downloads.

But times have changed. Each year audiences seem less willing to slog through a 40-page white paper, at least up front. They need to trust that the white papers and other collateral you develop to solve their content problems are worth their time. A major part of findability is building this trust with simpler, more accessible content.

Audiences need simple, straightforward answers to their questions. If you can take all the content out of a white paper and break it into discrete, snackable chunks that answer specific questions, and then serve those chunks to users when they need the answers in the format that works best for them, you will be solving the central problem of content marketing. You can't do this without an authoring environment that enables writers and editors to focus on answering those questions and building experiences that string together the answers in common user information paths. Eventually, you can present the whole paper, but you need to do it just one chapter or section at a time.

Simpler Sharing

Digital content has always been about sharing. The original use case of the web at CERN was to enable physicists to share information more quickly than they could with the traditional journal model, with its layers of review and perfectionism, not to mention printing and distribution. The first form of sharing was simply linking your research to other related research. And that model persists today for much web content.

Following the tradition started by Tim Berners-Lee, the innovators of the web have built systems like Twitter and Facebook to enhance the ability for users to share content. In measuring these systems, we have learned a great deal about the kinds of content that people share—and we have found that it's small, like short video clips or quotes. Only about .5% of users share pages by using the share buttons on pages. Most page sharing is done by simply copying and pasting the URL into a sharing tool such as HootSuite, shortening it, and writing a tweet or post that complements the link. This is called "dark social." According to Rio Social, a company that developed a way to track dark social, about 6% of users typically share pages in this way, on average. It's still a low number compared to snackable content. But pages do get shared in small numbers if they're well built—single purpose and authoritative.

White papers and other monolithic content doesn't get shared all that much. Since most companies create many web pages and white papers and not many small digital assets such as infographics, they suffer from a lack of social sharing.

Structured content can help solve this problem. A case study, for example, might contain a set of vital statistics on a company, a public profile of an interviewee, a pull quote, an infographic, and a video. Though few people would share the whole case study, they might be inclined to share some of those components and perhaps link back to the full study in their posts. This can work only if your case studies are chunked up and coded in parts that are assembled as web pages but shareable in chunks.

Increased Reuse

The larger the piece of content, the harder it is to reuse it in multiple related contexts. Because brands tend to create large white papers and other thought leadership pieces, they tend to create the same thing over and over again. IBM creates a CIO Study each year, which updates the previous year's finding of what's most important to a large sample of surveyed CIOs. It is one of IBM's most valuable pieces of content every year. It is one of our most valuable pieces of content. But much of it is just duplicated from the previous year. What if you could create reusable components and assemble them so that you only create the net new information each year and simply reuse the rest? What if you could serve it to your audience in this way, so that those who had read the previous reports got only the new stuff rather than needing to reread a very similar report every year with a few new things added? Structured content authoring solves reuse problems like this, reducing the amount of content you need to author by orders of magnitude.

More Adaptive

Another new requirement of digital content is that it serves the needs of the audience, regardless of the device used to consume it. Most sites that do this today use a process called *responsive design*. Responsive design automatically reformats content so that it fits the shape of the screen. A similar approach, *adaptive design*, selects from several different predefined screen sizes to optimally display the content. Both of these approaches take the same content and show it on screens of varying sizes, which is a neat trick.

But merely reformatting the same content for different screen sizes is not an ideal experience, especially for long-form content. As Karen McGrane wrote in her 2013 book *Content Strategy for Mobile*, "responsive design doesn't fix your content problem." Why not? Well, the more content you have on a page, the more readers need to scroll. This might be an experience users are willing to put up with now because everyone is building content this way, but if you ask them, they will say they prefer not to scroll. And for a variety of reasons, forcing them to scroll kills your success.

The smaller the device, the more important it is to give the essential information on the first or second screen. Responsive design alone tends to bury essential information because it is written for a laptop screen and reformatted for a phone or tablet. This is what Karen McGrane means when she says responsive design doesn't solve your content problem.

To solve your content problem, you need *adaptive content*. Adaptive content enables your content to be cut up into small pieces, tagged for device sensitivity, and served to the device as needed. With adaptive content, you can tag the most essential content in a piece to display first in a mobile device and in the third paragraph of a laptop screen. Why would you do this? Well, users have different scanning and reading habits on different devices. It only makes sense to display the content according to the reading order your audience prefers. Tuning the reading order of your content for the device requires adaptive content.

Adaptive content and responsive design are not mutually exclusive. In fact, they often work in tandem to create the best content experiences for your audiences. Tablets and phones come in various shapes and sizes. Adaptive content might specify the content tagged for each device type, while responsive design reshapes it for the particular phone or tablet it lands on.

More Personalized

The Holy Grail of data-driven marketing is one-to-one marketing: learning your individual audience members so well that you can create content as though you are having a conversation with each and every one of them. But instead of a chat interface that requires a person on both ends, on your end you are serving thousands of users at one time with just the content they need at that moment in their conversation—their information journey—automatically. There is no man behind the curtain. There's a machine that learns your audience needs and serves them, better and better over time, like a virtual sales person. Many CMOs have had this on their agendas for years. What has kept them from finding the Holy Grail of data-driven marketing is an authoring environment that can support this requirement. Structured content authoring environments have a chance to do this.

Better Content Testing

How do you know your audience information needs? The truth is, it's as much art as science. What you can do with the current keyword research and social listening tools is to make educated guesses about your target audience. You never really know until you publish stuff. The ideal is to publish multiple versions of the same thing and test the results. But you can't really do this effectively unless you can break your content into small pieces and serve them in different order, and sometimes with different wording.

Keyword research can tell you which words tend to resonate with your target audience. But what if you could try multiple semantic variations of those words and measure the results in real time, then adjust your content toward the words that actually work? Adaptive content solves this problem because it allows authors to tag content all the way down to the phrase level and substitute different phrases in different versions of the same content, then test the results. The machine learns your audience preferences over time, and you can feed this data back into your audience analysis systems for future use by every author in your enterprise, as part of their guided authoring experience.

So why aren't we doing it? A critical challenge of content transformation is the transition from existing unstructured content authoring environments to new structured authoring systems. When you sell the new systems, you will encounter resistance from those who don't understand the value and think the current systems work just fine. This section should help you address those doubters.

Traditionally, web content authoring environments came in two flavors: form-based systems and WYSIWYG (what you see is what you get) editors. Neither is particularly helpful. In form-based systems, authors typically write in Microsoft Word or some similar word processor, later needing to copy and paste the results into fields. The fields feed databases, which dump the content into templates onto web pages. One key problem (out of many) with form-based systems is that most of the editorial review happens in the word processing system, not in the form. And when it is published, the content and HTML live side by side. Making changes after publication requires HTML editors, who are typically not content people and who don't understand the content they're fixing. This process is slow and expensive.

WYSIWYG editors were built to solve the problems of form-based editors by allowing authors to write and publish content at the same time. Authors can get a sense of how their content will look before they publish it and make changes in the source as needed from the editor. The problem with WYSIWYG editors is that they focus on the page rather than the content. The author is advised to create content for a web page (typically assuming a browser the size of a laptop) and not for the audience, resulting in pages full of content, not all of which is useful and none of which is shareable or inherently adaptive to different devices. And the source of the content also doesn't separate the code from the words, so if you really need to fix something that involves both (say, an alt attribute or a CSS class), you are left with the same problem you had with the form-based systems.

Structured authoring environments solve these problems by separating the source from the content and helping authors build content for the audience—not necessarily for the page. When pages become just one output of a set of content modules, you can build systems of engagement with content that are much more adaptive, personalized, iterative, reusable, shareable, and findable. That's how you need to transform your authoring environment to meet the challenges of today's audiences.

Content Management Systems

A content management system (CMS) allows you to store, manage, and share content according to the needs of your audience. They are typically repositories of content generated by the authoring environment with clever mechanisms to ensure version control and minimize duplication. To the extent that your CMS can manage content modules and not merely pages, that's great. But can it do this in an intelligent way, incrementally improving over time?

Again, we don't want to wade into the technical details that separate different content management systems. But ask yourself whether your CMS is up to the modern task of content management on a couple of points.

Integrated Insights

Once a piece of content is in your content management database, the system needs a way of tagging it with the performance metrics it gathers over time. Take the case study example. Perhaps you determine that the most shared aspect of a case study is a video, a fact you learn because the system (YouTube) that measures engagement with the videos also feeds that data into the CMS, attaching the engagement data to that particular video. This might help you, for example, put the video rather than the infographic on the first phone screen.

The point is that your CMS must have an API for each of your data sources, which together build an effectiveness score for each piece of content. These insights need to be accessible to anyone who might want to reuse that piece of content based on its prior effectiveness. As mentioned earlier, it is particularly important to have these insights baked into the authoring system, so that authors can share and reuse content based on its effectiveness to the audience.

Integrated Governance

The larger your organization, the more critical it is that your CMS has built-in logic to ensure that you don't create duplicate experiences. Users are rightfully confused by multiple versions of content solving the same problem or answering the same question.

But in large, siloed, organizations, this duplication is very common, due to lack of governance. Most CMSs enable authors or editors to check in or check out pieces of content, to ensure that there aren't multiple versions of the very same piece floating around and creating confusion about what is the definitive copy.

Governance takes this to another level. It doesn't just ensure that you don't create duplicate copies; it ensures that you don't create new content that duplicates what is already working for users. Two pieces of content could have radically different designs or lengths but be about the same topic. An adequate governance system reduces duplicate content at the topic level, not just the file level. When you combine this concept with structured content strategy, you can reduce the amount of content you create by up to 90%. This saves money, of course. But it also leads to better customer experiences.

The good news is, content management systems are probably the most mature parts of the content marketing infrastructure. So no matter which system you choose, chances are it will meet most of your needs.

Taxonomy and Tagging Systems

Taxonomies are important because they help us speak our customers' language and help us organize our content in common ways. When we tag content with centrally controlled values, we help content management systems and other applications serve more relevant content to our audiences.

But using the *T* word often causes executives' eyes to glaze over and prompts those execs to start remembering meetings that they are already late for. Please don't close the book yet. Taxonomy management is really not that hard.

A taxonomy is all about naming things as a company. That is a central part of marketing. If you asked brand marketers if naming products is essential, they would of course say yes. A taxonomy just organizes these names, making it possible to understand how two names are related, which is especially important when a name needs to change. Most importantly, taxonomies help us name things *consistently*.

You allow taxonomies to do their job when you follow three essential approaches:

- *Use data to decide wording.* When we have debates about wording, we get sucked into the maelstrom of subjective semantics. If your taxonomy systems are informed by data rather than opinion, debates don't regress; they are informed by the data. A taxonomy is just a mapping between the common words in our vocabulary and the way we want to put our stamp on them in our corporate nomenclature. If the core word you use comes from an external data source, such as keyword research or an accepted industry classification scheme, arguments about semantics evaporate. Also, external data sources tend to change less often than brand names. For these reasons, data-driven taxonomies are easier to manage and more effective.

- *Use ontologies to organize your taxonomies.* An ontology describes the relationships between different names in a taxonomy rather than the meanings of the names themselves. Ontologies are as to links as taxonomies are to pages. Links provide context for web pages, so that Google can understand the purpose and relative authority of a page in context. Similarly, if you use ontologies, you won't have to focus so much on the meaning of individual names, and you can build relationships between related names to use different names in different contexts.

The mappings between core data-driven words and corporate brand names are examples of ontologies.

■ *Use objects, not rigid hierarchies.* We have a natural tendency to want to build hierarchies of names: Products go up to brands, brands go up to categories, and so on. The problem is that a lot of names fit under multiple branches of a tree. Is cloud security under the cloud category or the security category? The correct answer is "yes." But hierarchies force us to choose to put them in either one branch or another—or have multiple variations of the same value. Object-oriented ontologies solve this problem by focusing on relationships that are not hierarchical. These relationships become part of the intelligence that you build into each node of your taxonomy.

It's not easy. But if you know what kind of tools you need and you hire really smart people to use them, you can have a taxonomy that works for your digital content efforts. When we say it works, we mean it is relatively easy for authors to use the appropriate tags for their content. When they do, it's possible to build adaptive, personalized, iterative, reusable, shareable, and findable content. Without good tagging, it's virtually impossible to do any of this.

Audience Feedback Systems

Systems that measure the performance of your content are perhaps the most mature of the three types of systems that you need to integrate. But that doesn't mean it's any easier to integrate them into your content ecosystem. Because feedback systems have been around so long, you are probably already drowning in relatively big data and can't figure out what to focus on. Just when you think you get a handle on it, you get another deluge, as the data comes at you faster and faster, as the executives demand that you analyze it in real time. The biggest requirement for your audience feedback system is probably simplification.

Simplification really is possible. Most marketers do not need to understand the complexities of all the different measurement systems out there. It was once a simpler life for marketers, when all they needed to understand was their web analytics system. And as long as all of your content was on your website, that's all marketers needed.

But with social media quickly moving from a technical curiosity to a marketing imperative, more analytics systems loom. Suddenly every social platform where you want to place and promote your content has its own lovely little analytics system. Twitter, Facebook, LinkedIn, YouTube—you name it—they all have separate analytics systems that track Likes and clicks and many other metrics.

Rather than pulling all these metrics in and trying to analyze them together, you need to understand your key performance indicators (KPIs) by which you will measure the results of all your efforts. KPIs are like filters for data that allow you to simplify the data that comes in and analyze it when it does. KPIs are up next.

Key Performance Indicators

Key performance indicators are the foundation of an analytics strategy. What you choose to measure will determine every other decision you make in designing a system that works. In Chapter 2, we took a quick look at the different types of measurements that your analyst might suggest to you. Here we want to give you a simplified model that you can give to any analyst to help them understand what you need to know:

- *Impressions.* Your first question for any piece of marketing is "Did they see it?" For some kinds of content, such as a blog post or a web page, your web analytics system probably does a great job of giving you this number (which it calls page views). YouTube dutifully reports the number of views of your video. But for other kinds of content, such as tweets or Facebook shares, we know how many people could have seen it but not always how many did. For emails, you might need to settle for knowing how many people opened your email. Nevertheless, when you can determine how many people saw your content, it's a number worth knowing.

- *Selections.* Your next question for any piece of marketing is "Did they choose it?" Whether it was clicked with a mouse or stabbed with a finger, you want to know how often people engaged with your content by going deeper than just seeing it. Most kinds of content can be measured this way, and when it can, it tells you which content is resonating.

- *Conversions.* Your next question is "Did it persuade them?" Exactly what your conversion is will vary by your business, but whether you want to see an online shopping cart checkout or white paper download, you want to know which content is being seen by the people who end up converting.

- *Revenue.* Your next question is "How much did we sell?" For ecommerce, this is a simple calculation, but you might need more help to determine offline sales by tying your online conversions to a point-of-sale coupon or a customer relationship management (CRM) lead, for example. In any case, your analyst is the one who can help you connect the dots.

- *Return on Investment (ROI).* Your final question is "Was it worth it?" Most marketers know how much they spend, but they don't know how much they make. If you can crack the revenue question, you can calculate your ROI to prove that what you are doing is effective.

Your KPIs are critical to running content marketing as a business, but it isn't the only feedback that you need to collect. In addition to knowing how you are doing, you need other numbers to help you understand exactly which content asset got (or didn't get) the results you were hoping for. *Attribution modeling* is up next.

Attribution Modeling

Many buyer journeys require several pieces of content before the prospect is ready to talk to a sales rep or directly purchase a product. In those cases, each piece of content plays some role in the purchase and should get some credit for it. *Attribution* is about assessing the relative contribution to revenue for each individual piece of content.

Attribution is an old concept that goes back to offline direct marketing, when *matchback systems* tried to determine what percentage of credit for a sale different individual catalog mailings should receive. It made sense to them that if it takes multiple viewings of ads to persuade consumers to act, then being exposed to the same products month after month must have some cumulative effect also. Many studies were done to understand how to put together a matchback model with the best calculation to attribute credit. For digital marketing, we still use models to do this, but we call them *attribution models*.

Some attribution models give stronger weight to the early-stage content because it is what brings the customer into the digital front door in the first place. Some attribution models ascribe greater weight to the piece of content immediately prior to purchase because it is the "closer." And there are models that give equal weight to each piece.

Whatever attribution model you choose, its accuracy depends on measurement systems that track users through the buyer journey. As we examined the plethora of analytics systems above, it's critical that your marketing analyst know how to automatically pass the baton from system to system so that you know that the user who looked at your YouTube video is the same user who is now visiting your website.

Several methods can tie visitor data across systems, including cookies, tracking codes, and device identifiers. Which ones make sense will likely depend on the situation you find yourself in; you will unfortunately find some situations in which none will help. Impress upon your analyst the criticality of tying as many individual paths through social networks, search, and all the way through purchase—even offline purchase. The fanciest attribution model on the planet is limited by the inability to chain visitor data across audience feedback systems.

As you become more sophisticated in your use of attribution modeling, you will find that these systems can do more than just give content credit for the part they play in purchase decisions; they help you understand your user paths so that you can optimize them. In this way, they are both reporting mechanisms and diagnostics that can help you present common next steps. Think of how Amazon presents products that are typically purchased together; much like that, if you know frequent paths through content, you can recommend common next steps to users to ease their paths through your content.

Wrapping Up: Your Entire Infrastructure Matters

The purpose of this chapter is to get you thinking about how to transform your marketing content infrastructure to enable outside-in marketing. It is not to help you make actual technology decisions. Leave those evaluations to the techies who specialize in the systems. But you need to know enough to validate their recommendations when they come in. You can use this chapter as a playbook for such evaluations to ensure that your content marketers have the tools they need to build outside-in marketing content.

As you work with your technology team to transform your content marketing systems, you might be tempted to focus on the systems that you are personally using (the content authoring and management systems) to the exclusion of the audience research and audience feedback systems.

Unfortunately, much of that money has been squandered on harder-to-use content messaging systems that lack the ability to create the new structured content required. We fear that in an effort to right that wrong, we might miss the need to also invest in the consistently undercapitalized audience research and feedback systems. Most companies have overspent on the wrong content messaging technologies, buying fancy multimedia authoring tools and content management systems while starving the data side of the business.

As you consider your technology investments, remember that fishing in the right lake and being able to count how many you caught will likely get you a lot more money to invest in better fishing equipment than if you ignore those areas.

In the next chapter, we'll drill down on content strategy—especially focusing on the buyer journey as the most critical prism through which to view your content decisions.

ROB KEY, ON HOW SOCIAL MEDIA
CAN BE ANALYZED AS BIG DATA

Rob Key is founder and CEO of leading social consultancy Converseon (Converseon.com) and holds the same roles with its sister social analytics software company, Revealed Context (RevealedContext.com).

Many people are talking about big data, but you're someone who's actually doing something about it. How do you help clients gain insights from all the social conversation out there?

The promise of big data remains largely that in many cases—a promise. The key challenge to unlock the value of big data is really about getting to the right data, quickly and efficiently, to generate meaningful insight and then get it into the hands of the people who can make use of it in near real time—whether through predictive analytics, business intelligence, or more programmatic approaches, such as programmatic advertising.

With the explosion of social conversation data, this advanced filtering is essential, requiring moving away from the widespread but primitive Boolean keyword queries to a machine learning approach that rapidly learns from humans' interactions. We need to find those proverbial needles in the haystack, just as more and more hay is being stacked on the pile.

In research we've done at Converseon, most Boolean queries attain just 15%–30% relevancy, especially for brands with ambiguous keywords such as "Sprint." Accounting for the complexities of how a relevant conversation might be expressed is far beyond human ability to program a Boolean query. Add an extra word here, and all of a sudden you have a massive irrelevant data set; remove a word, and you then miss important information that *is* relevant. When combining low relevancy in the data with other filtering and analysis challenges, such as automated sentiment using rules-based approaches that attain often only 60% accuracy, you simply cannot mainstream this data with confidence or apply it to the areas that companies are demanding—such as predictive analytics.

The good news is this is changing fast. Techniques that use machine and deep learning that keep humans in the loop to adjust the algorithms (techniques we use at Converseon and Revealed Context) actually have been shown in independent tests to attain near-human precision and to rapidly increase relevancy to 90%. When data hits this level of quality, it has been proven to have those critical predictive capabilities needed to fully mainstream this data across company operations.

Big data might be cool, but accurate and meaningful data is what matters—and these technologies have evolved to now allow vast analysis of big data in accurate and meaningful ways. But you have to get the data right first. Too many organizations have tried to do the opposite—go big and then try to tune it.

What do you see as the best ways for social media to inform companies on what content they should be producing?

We now have vast storage of conversations over years that can be analyzed, reanalyzed, and trended in increasingly sophisticated ways. Some have referred to Twitter as a cultural assessment tool, but the expression of language, ideas, thoughts, opinions, goes far beyond Twitter and is, in fact, evolving every day.

In fact, the advent of social platforms is accelerating the evolution of language, such as neologisms. New slang arises daily and spreads almost instantaneously. There are more than 2,000 words added daily to the urban dictionary, for example. Among all cultures, language has helped groups understand and assess who is "part of the tribe" and who isn't. Language binds people and culture.

So we now have the largest library of language evolution at our fingertips, allowing us to trace lineages of language among specific groups. We know how language differs between demographic groups, regional groups, and those who share similar interests. If brands want to deeply connect to their customers, peers, and other constituents, it all begins with *language*. Traditional search keyword tools provide mere surface analysis.

Social listening can dive deep—sentiment, emotion, intensity, phrases, slang, sarcasm, unmet needs, and more. Once one maps these conversations across time, geographies, and segments or audiences, the most obvious place to apply it is within content strategies that engage where these conversations are happening and then, of course, through "owned" content strategies—such as websites through search engine optimization. But these conversations evolve quickly, so brands must listen intently and generate content efficiently and effectively if they want to stay relevant to these conversations.

There's nothing worse than a brand diving headfirst into a conversation that is already considered *passé* in online environments, which happens far too often. To adapt quickly to changing topics requires streamlining content approaches. That viral off-the-cuff Super Bowl tweet is fine and good, but staffing an entire command center full of lawyers, compliance officers, producers, creatives, community managers to produce one tweet is beyond the means of most brands.

How does influencer marketing intersect with content marketing, and what does social have to do with that?

It's been well documented by others that only a relatively small number of those participating in social media produce any actual real content. The vast majority are simply lurkers—reading, and perhaps passing along, content others create. This reality creates a dark social web of interactions with content that requires other means to elicit insight into how those audiences are reacting to your content. The most promiscuous content creators tend to have an outsized influence on key conversations and opinions. Even before the explosion of social media, researchers have shown that it's only about 10% of people who influence the opinions of the other 90%. In social media that number of influencers might even be 2%–3%.

So it's critical to understand who those key influencers are within a specific category. The mistakes most brands make regarding influencers fall into two categories.

First, they use primitive metrics to identify who is influential. An academic last year reverse-engineered a popular influence algorithm and found it was heavily Twitter-based and was essentially counting only basic vanity metrics such as followers and re-tweets. They might be loud, but that does not mean they influence. Real influence identification requires a more in-depth approach that looks at the totality of the social conversation but also measures other factors, including offline data sets—are they, for example, referred to frequently by others, even if they don't tweet or create social content themselves frequently?

The second mistake is that they then listen to only a sliver of what these influencers say or do, generally as it relates to them. These are not media conduits—they are people with broad interests and ideas that are fluid and change. And, in many cases, they want to be engaged with to solicit their ideas as much as you share your ideas.

The best relationships are often formed when individuals get together to take on a common task. Relationships are not often effectively formed if one speaks "at" another—especially someone who is influential and well respected in their field. The concept of co-creation with key influencers is a powerful one.

But it begins by listening and understanding the full individual. New approaches—such as what we do—look at the full conversations and activities of a potential influencer to understand them on a broader level. Yes, they might be influential in cloud computing, but they might also love dogs. We now have the ability to understand that, so we can create content and engage opportunities that connect on that more fundamental, human level.

In the sprint to monetize social, we have to take a step back again and not forget social is comprised of individuals.

What trends in privacy do you see affecting the way data can be collected?

There was a day when most social conversation was public and freely available. There is a movement now toward more private communities, peer sharing platforms, and behind-the-firewall discussions. It's a natural evolution but one that can make social listening increasingly challenging. I hope there is a continued recognition of the importance of broadly available and searchable expressions of opinions in a world where far too many people are entering their own echo chambers by tuning in only to people who share their opinion.

The cross-pollination of ideas matters today more than ever. And it's public conversation that drives that.

That said, the rise of private conversations—whether within private platforms or within the brand organizations themselves (such as call center and other "voice of customer" data) means that those advanced text analytic filters that can make meaningful sense of the conversations are going to have to be more deeply integrated upstream and sometimes within the firewalls of an organization or specific app—essentially preprocessing it in a way that protects the privacy of individuals.

The good news is that with the advent of more sophisticated APIs and other "plug-in" techniques, this can be done quite easily. The core challenge is ensuring that multiple analytics tools and filters—each of which might measure things differently—don't create a cacophony of analysis. There has to be one truth within organizations for consistency to avoid false conclusions and to ensure all of the data can be rolled up into one place. The danger is if different applications and platforms adopt their own approaches and frameworks, there will be no way to piece it all back together into a coherent story—and with little to no ability to validate the information. What I hope for, and advocate, is that platforms work with key brands to allow them to plug in their own filters so the value of the data can remain consistent and useful.

Whether it's the advent of mobile, lack of time, or some other reason, social sharing seems to be trending to smaller bites of content, whether it is blogs shrinking to tweets or video lengths dropping to as little as a few seconds. How does that affect brands?

Our attention spans are getting shorter—dramatically so. Brands have tried to adapt by becoming media companies that first leverage social data for insight but then produce content in multiple formats (text, audio, images, video) and in the formats and durations required by the platforms. It's not a simple thing but certainly requires getting to the point more quickly. The art movement had a minimalist movement in the '70s. We can learn a bit from them. Less can be more. But it also requires building a content capability inside the brand and avoiding some of the more traditional agency-driven content approaches that simply require jumping through too many hoops for approval to stay relevant to the conversation.

Do you see differences in the way large companies need to work with social data as opposed to how small companies can operate?

Many large companies measure different things in different ways—often inconsistently. This is a core challenge. Some companies use multiple listening platforms, for example, but each platform analyzes sentiment differently. Rolling that data up into anything meaningful then becomes impossible.

Mainstreaming the data with confidence into critical operations—such as business intelligence, product development, and more—becomes even a greater challenge. Unlike at smaller companies, the most successful social data initiatives at large brands embrace the data tree analogy—one "trunk" of data flow that is tuned specifically to a brand for the highest recall, precision, and relevancy. This trunk includes what we call "custom classifiers" unique to their business to really understand the data in more critical ways to categorize and isolate data rapidly and effectively so that it can be "branched off" into various business operations.

This way, the organization can be assured that, while different parts of the organization may be viewing different data sets, it's all coming from the same source, and it's annotated and filtered in a consistent manner so that it all rolls up together in a meaningful way. This also means that simple off-the-shelf text analytics often won't do the job. The solutions need to be tuned to specific brands and industries. The word "small," for example, might be good if selling smart phones but not so good if selling hotel rooms.

The newest approaches—such as those we do at Revealed Context—allow for this specific brand and domain tuning. The industry sometimes focuses too much on tools, where, in my view, it's the data layer that is the critical piece. In an API economy, consistent data can flow by and between different tools. Getting this data layer right is the key.

What trends do you see in social analytics over the next few years?

Social data will no longer be isolated but instead will be mainstreamed into organizations and will touch many different areas of operations—marketing, customer service, product development, innovation, and more. This has always been the promise of social data, but until now the data was simply not good enough to mainstream with confidence. The breakthrough has been the new technologies that generate the precision and analysis needed to get the buy-in necessary. With more and more research coming out showing the power of social data, it provides increasing validation and confidence to fully leverage it.

But social data will not remain in a vacuum. It will be integrated with other voice-of-customer data in new and interesting ways so that all customer input, feedback, and opinion is captured, filtered, and acted on rapidly.

It will also be a key input into broader measurement and BI frameworks so that correlations can be understood and adjustments can be made that truly improve business performance. The fixation on tools will give way to a deeper fixation on the data layer. The free flow of this data will increase between tools and applications, within and outside the walls of organizations. This data will be part of the plumbing of organizations and, by integrating it programmatically into more and more activities (such as programmatic advertising and CRM systems), will become second nature to many. It will become an increasingly key intelligence component embedded within all parts of the organization. And that's when the power of social data will truly be unlocked.

5

Content Strategy: Aligning Content to the Buyer Journey

"Can you describe your company's differentiation to us?"

Three executives from a successful regional chain of mattress stores shifted uncomfortably in their seats, until the boss confidently blurted out, "We have the widest selection, the lowest prices, and the best service."

"So, you have the most mattresses of anyone?"

"Well, probably not, but we have plenty," the boss answered, seeming to lose some confidence.

"And nobody underprices you?"

"Well, just those online guys. Our prices are competitive with other stores around here."

Competitive doesn't sound like the *lowest* price, and we were discussing the content marketing strategy for the company, so the fact that "those online guys" were priced lower didn't sound terribly differentiating. Still, we pressed on, seemingly to the inevitable. "And how do you know that you have the best service?"

"Well, nobody complains."

The truth is that this successful company was differentiated the way many are: They were the best choice in a local area. No one wants to drive 30 miles with a mattress on their roof, so close is good. Unfortunately, on the web, every company is equally close, and they deliver anywhere. This company didn't really have a differentiation that translates to content marketing.

After a lot of discussion, we realized that several of their stores do a booming business in hypo-allergenic mattresses and associated products, such as mattress covers that keep out dust mites, down-free pillows, and many other products. Two sales associates with allergic children had done a ton of research and even gotten referrals from local allergists. Now, *that's* a differentiated content strategy.

And, as you'll see in this chapter, understanding your differentiation can help you focus your efforts on the right buyer journey. The buyer journey for buying a mattress is extremely competitive and probably would not end well for this retailer. On the other hand, the buyer journey for addressing a child's allergy might end really well, especially if one of the doctors was willing to be part of the marketing.

This is the strategy at the heart of content marketing—finding the differentiation that leads to a compelling story, and telling that story in a way that aligns to the buyer journey. Executing such a strategy isn't always easy, and we can't say that this retailer lived happily ever after because of its strategy, but executing an undifferentiated strategy is a recipe for failure. But it's not the only factor in failure. The truth is that few companies execute content marketing well—for several reasons. You need to clear these blockers at your company to execute your strategy:

- *Mistaking volume for effectiveness.* Most of our clients think they need to constantly create new content to set the brand agenda on the web. The reality is quite the opposite: Companies that build evergreen content that serves persistent client needs have more success. Those that treat web content like a magazine—to be created, published, and discarded—merely clutter their websites, confusing their clients and prospects. Better to constantly update and freshen the evergreen content that is already working than to continue to dump new stuff out there for no good reason.

  Executives who succeed at content marketing imitate land development. Perhaps you build a hotel on a site. Then you landscape it. Then you continually beautify it and maintain it as a pleasing destination, adding small gestures to delight your customers. That's what websites are: destinations that delight prospects and clients with continuous improvements.

- *Too much top-down control.* Too many executives at our client sites think of web content as if it is ad copy—something to be scrutinized and reviewed to death prior to publishing. They don't hand control of the product to their content teams—the experts at building client experiences. And once they have reviewed and approved the product, they don't like changes. Web content marketing must be agile, allowing teams to iteratively improve the product over long periods of time.

  Executives who succeed at content marketing only care about the KPIs the efforts drive (conversions, leads, revenue, etc.). They let teams build content that works to deliver those results. They don't micromanage the product team. The team controls the content and is responsible for the results.

- *Too few resources.* Some of our clients labor under the myth that web content is easier than print, so it should require fewer resources. It's actually the opposite, due to the interconnectedness of content. Magazine content exists in a vacuum. If you have a bad issue of a magazine, no big whoop. Make a better one next week or next month. If you let a microsite go off the rails with inexperienced resources, it could take six months to recover in a competitive marketplace. One bad microsite can pull down the domain authority of the whole site.

- *Too much fragmentation.* Most of our clients lack central standards and oversight for web content. A company of any size and complexity that's in this boat presents itself as a loose federation of disconnected microsites rather than a single coordinated site. This makes the client experience poor, with dead ends and too many irrelevant links.

  Standards and governance help all product teams collaboratively produce client experiences that work. It is the hard work of content strategy, but it is absolutely necessary.

- *Overreliance on agencies.* Most of our clients outsource their marketing content efforts to agencies, which are even less connected to whatever central standards and governance processes exist. Because these agencies often get paid for volume rather than results, they overproduce as a matter of course.

  There are lots of reasons to outsource parts of the whole ecosystem of content marketing. Because the parts of this ecosystem are typically run by different agencies, or parts of a larger agency, the whole ecosystem will tend to get fragmented without a centralized strategy to organize the whole, prioritize efforts, and govern the activities. Again, this tends to mean more in-house resources than executives are comfortable with. But outsourcing your strategy is a recipe for disaster, especially if you use multiple agencies.

Many companies have not updated their approach to content strategy to cope with the demands of digital marketing. Old-time content strategies were born in print; the agency created glossy brochures and other collateral to be distributed at trade shows and in sales calls. When they tried to use the same strategy on the web, it broke their websites. Now they seek a sustainable content strategy built for the web.

Our contention throughout this book is that proper content marketing strategy focuses on inbound marketing rather than the traditional advertising content of outbound marketing. We have nothing against advertising, but this book focuses on something better.

In this chapter, we do a deeper dive into buyer journeys, which focus on exactly what the audience needs at the moment it needs it. Buyer journeys aren't linear paths—every buyer backtracks and makes a singular path through the content—but buyer journeys are a good model for a common way through the content.

Top-Down Content Strategy

Top-down content strategy is the process of finding the keywords and phrases your target audience most often searches for and building the content that answers their implicit questions. That sounds a lot like our description of outside-in content marketing, doesn't it? Well, it is. You see, the words your target audiences primarily search for will tend to be top-of-funnel words. They have a high demand in Google for a reason: A lot of people search for them. They also tend to be broad categories; the more people search for a keyword, the broader it is. Brand terms can also have high demand, but you have to really mess up to avoid being found for your branded keywords. Your top-of-funnel opportunities will be high-volume *unbranded* keywords.

Sheer volume is not the only criterion for figuring out your most important top-of-funnel keywords; it's not even the most important. Most important is *relevance* to your target audience. Your target audience is looking for your areas of differentiation—in other words, which keywords your company has the credibility to win.

Briefly, if you have a *right to win*, your company *belongs* near the top of the search results for a keyword. Google really needs to show your content because your company is a reputable source of content for the implied question posed by the searcher. How your company differentiates itself from its competition determines your right to win. Finding those high-demand opportunities for which you have a right to win is the first step in building a top-down content strategy.

Google gives brands credit for having competitive advantages in the marketplace. For example, most people who search for the keyword *smart phone* want either an iPhone or an Android device, so top search results show the top providers in those two categories. Who earns top position is largely dependent on content. All things considered, content experiences that succinctly answer the questions implicit in the queries will win better ranking position. But if you don't make a competitive product in that category, the best content in the world won't help you win for that keyword.

One place to start is studying the search results for your top-of-funnel keywords. Suppose your content doesn't rank well for those keywords and your competitors' content does. What might be wrong is that your content isn't as strong as your competitors', but it could also be about your product's differentiation in the market.

Your top content opportunities are those that have high audience interest where your company is in a unique position to win the market. Every industry has at least one well-respected source on where competitors stand. Gartner can show your tech company toward the upper right of its Magic Quadrant. J.D. Power can award your product for quality. Yelp can show off your five-star reviews.

This is one of the reasons Google uses links as a ranking factor. If a lot of authoritative sites link to your site in reference to a product or service category, it's an indicator that you are a market leader. When these impartial arbiters declare your product a winner, it is because it is differentiated for some specific problem or some specific audience.

Auditing Existing Content

Once you have a prioritized list of content opportunities, it's time to find the content you already have for those opportunities and assess its effectiveness; this is *content auditing*.

Some experts conduct content audits by crawling and cataloging your entire site, then assessing the whole corpus of information. We don't find this approach particularly helpful for medium and large websites because only a small percentage of your content (often 10% or less) garners the lion's share of the traffic, so that is where you should start.

The way to identify this high-value content is to start, once again, with Google. Google Search Console (formerly known as Google Webmaster

---

WHY NOT A BOTTOM-UP CONTENT STRATEGY?

The pressure for most marketing organizations is to start at the bottom of the funnel because they need results, and it's easiest to prove results at the bottom of the funnel. If a typical buyer journey has five steps, optimizing the purchase of the product in the fifth step will get the immediate attention of most organizations.

Why? Lack of measurement.

Sure, it's easiest to measure the last touch of a buyer journey, but is it the most *important* touch in that journey? Is it the page that most strongly influenced the buyer to purchase? Chances are the purchase or conversion experience is not the most important. Chances are there was some content closer to the top of the funnel that triggered the buyer to convert or purchase. In long buyer journeys, oftentimes a series of steps contribute equally to the purchase. If you're not measuring how content influences buyer behavior in the whole funnel, you'll never discover that. And you'll end up putting most of your efforts into helping customers who would have purchased from you anyway.

Starting at the bottom for your strategy leads to other problems as you work your way higher up. Let's say you start at product pages where customers purchase or convert. Your next step would be to go one level up in the funnel. Now you must collaborate with the owners of different product pages to help the customer make the right decision

Tools) can show all of your indexed content, prioritized by the most popular keywords that draw searchers to that content. Search Console provides a wealth of information on those critical pages, revealing their absolute ranking, impressions, clicks, and any technical crawling issues with the pages. While you can examine Search Console directly, many SEO optimization tools check your Search Console account each day to capture the metrics and show you the critical trends for your pages.

You're probably convinced at this point that Google is an excellent source of information on the content that's *working*. But how do you identify potentially valuable content that isn't working yet? Of course, you have your web analytics package to measure your audience's interaction with your content. And there are auditing tools that find writing errors, suggest new

---

between several different products. All too often, this leads to internal conflicts, where product owners end up jockeying for position on that page to entice more clicks to their own products. This can be fatal to the client experience because you've turned a potentially outside-in approach to an internal tug-of-war. What the customer wants is lost.

There is a better way. If you start at the top of the funnel to build experiences that help prospects learn about your unique position in the marketplace, you can build experiences for the client first. Only after you know you are building outside-in content marketing do you worry quite so much about making sure they ultimately get to good purchasing experiences.

DB Squared, a B2B finance company that sells refactoring and other cash-flow services, hired a single marketing person and increased their web page views by more than 300% by focusing on top-of-funnel lead generation through content marketing. By focusing on quality content assets targeted to the beginning of the buyer journey, that single marketing person avoided diluting her impact over a large number of activities and concentrated on the area where content marketing can help the most.

There's nothing wrong with starting an optimization effort at the bottom of the funnel if you desperately need to show marketing results quickly. But don't mistake that as a content strategy. Your strategy needs to start from the top.

headlines or calls to action, and generally help you improve your content. You should also be using A/B or multivariate testing. What works in those tests can guide you more broadly for your content strategy.

Ultimately, your goal in performing any type of content audit is to understand the following:

- Which content is worth keeping and optimizing
- Which content you should delete and redirect to a new experience
- What new content is required to fill gaps
- How all this content fits into a strategy that serves your audiences
- Where your content fits into typical buyer journeys

Of all these important points, the most important is typically your buyer journeys, which is what we tackle next.

IS THERE DIFFERENTIATION THAT CONTENT MARKETING DOESN'T WORK FOR?

It's sad but true: Content marketing doesn't work for every kind of business. You remember our friends at the retail mattress chain? Even if they wanted to pursue their original ideas for differentiation (selection, price, and service), content marketing would be a hard way to do it.

It's not that no one is known for the widest selection of products. (Does Amazon pop into your mind?) Other companies might have that reputation within their niches, too, ranging from big names such as Home Depot to small lighting retailer 1000bulbs.com. Each of them has staked their reputation on selection, but it's not necessarily easy to prove your wide selection with content marketing.

Similarly, Walmart is known for the lowest prices, making it hard for anyone else to be there, too, because there is only one winner. Still, you might think of discounters within several niche businesses. Unfortunately, it's not easy to think of what kind of content would prove you have the lowest prices.

Service is similar because it's hard to prove good service by talking about yourself. Review sites are popular for assuring good service, but

Mapping Buyer Journeys

The process of journey mapping usually starts in an organization as more of an art than a science, with sales reps outlining what a typical buyer or buying group looks like, then building personas for these buyers that focus on the information needs of buyers. Most companies stop there, but this process so far is based more on opinion than data. We advocate a more data-driven approach to journey mapping.

Using Search to Understand Buyer Journeys

If you start with a list of personas mapped to buying agendas, you can make the data much more meaningful by looking at typical search journeys of the personas in the list. It starts with your top keyword opportunities.

---

people can only check you on a review site when they have already found you. How do they find you if content marketing isn't a strong way to highlight good service?

The problem with each of these differentiators is that no one searches for *widest selection* or *lowest price* or *best service* because they know they won't find anything useful. Some kinds of differentiation are hard to sell through content marketing. The fact that they exist in real life will help you *retain* customers, but you need to find other differentiated areas to *attract* customers.

Sometimes, particular industries have even deeper problems. In the software business, it can be truly valuable to customers if your software products work together as a set of *solutions* or as a software *ecosystem*; often vendors provide volume discounts and can simplify integration work. Frequently, two separate products are not individual winners but might be the best solution when used together. You might notice similar limits to content marketing in your industry.

Regardless of your business, you must think clearly about how content tells the story of your differentiation in order for content marketing to work. Differentiation is where you start, but differentiation with a content marketing story is where you need to end up.

When building a content strategy from the top down, you can use the opportunities list as the first few steps in buyer journeys.

Even when you try to be data driven, you usually need to start with opinion, but let's dress it up and make it sound scientific: You start with a hypothesis. You might start with a hypothesis that the target persona will start the buyer journey by searching with a particular keyword. And you test your hypothesis against actual search results. Let's look at a real-life example that should be interesting to you, given that you are reading this book.

Say that Janet, a CMO who is relatively new to digital marketing (that's the persona), searches for the word *big data* (that's the hypothesis). Our data shows us that the implicit question Janet is asking is "What is big data?" That data consists of the first page of search results in Google, where several of the top results have that exact question in the title. This is the *Learn* step in the buyer journey.

Next, Janet begins the *Compare* step of her buyer journey by searching for *big data platforms*, resulting in Google showing several examples of third-party research sites, along with a few big data vendors. These pages compare the top platforms for managing big data. From this, she can make a list of the top vendors.

With Janet making some headway toward selecting a vendor, she starts the *Solve* step in her journey, trying to imagine what form a solution to the problem would take. Perhaps our keyword research data reveals that Janet searches for *components of a big data platform*. The pages she gets back from Google are geared more toward data architects than CMOs. For example, there is a white paper titled "An Enterprise Architect's Guide to Oracle's Big Data Platform" near the top of the search results. This suggests that we have another persona in play—software architect, who will be called in next to help complete the research on this potential purchase. When the answers to Janet's questions get too technical, she needs help. Again, the search results shown in response to these targeted keywords from our strategy form the data that reveals these facts.

It's likely that when Janet is confronted with these overly technical responses, she makes a note to ask a more technical person for help, but she probably also backtracks in the process, perhaps even back to the *Learn* stage to reground her understanding. Perhaps she returns to a more basic keyword, such as *big data for marketing*. Near the top of the results is the title "The CMO's Guide to Big Data." Bingo. Now Janet is on the right track.

Eventually, she gets to the point of being ready to start the purchase process, perhaps with an RFP. Her journey might take weeks or months, depending on the scale of what she needs to buy. Not all of her journey happens through search. But we assume for simplicity's sake that it does, so that we can build content that meets *her* needs—*and* those of her buying group—at each stage in her journey.

When you are testing the keywords your personas might use in their buyer journeys, there are no bad results. Eliminating irrelevant keywords from the list or assigning them to other personas is as valuable as confirming that the keywords fit the buying process for that persona.

At a certain point, you chart your buyers' courses through Google by connecting the dots of their individual keywords. Don't worry so much about the order of the keywords because your buyers will take nonlinear paths through the information. The data will help you prioritize which keywords opportunities bring the highest ROI. So we focus on the higher-demand keywords first and build the content architecture below using the buyer journeys as guides.

One critical thing to remember is that buyers do not typically take all the steps at one time. If someone is in the *Learn* stage, offering them free shipping for a product they don't even understand will not be effective. Your best outcome for each stage of the buyer journey is to move the buyer to the next stage. Buyers are not typically tolerant of offers unless they are ready to buy. Don't short-circuit the process to try to push buyers to move faster than they are willing to go.

Prioritizing Content Efforts

Perhaps it seems obvious that you should prioritize your content based on the potential ROI. But, while ROI seems like the obvious criterion to use for prioritization, it's not the only thing you should consider.

In many cases, time to market is just as important as ROI. Study your audit to determine which opportunities have existing content that merely needs to be optimized. The pages for which you rank on the second page in Google are your low-hanging fruit. Optimizing existing content might get you to the first page of the search results in a matter of days, while creating new content for the top of the funnel might take months to pay off. You have to do both, but it is always good to get a few quick wins while you are identifying the longer-term plays.

While ROI and time to market are both important criteria for prioritizing your content efforts, don't ignore your user experience. We will take a deep dive into user experience in Chapter 6, but we need to mention it here because you can't cherry-pick your keywords if doing so leaves gaps in the user experience. The simplest example of this problem is if you are creating a new microsite. You need to create the home page for the overall category for the microsite even if that particular concept doesn't correspond to a high-priority keyword. You wouldn't want to build several orphan pages just because those deeper keywords offer the highest ROI.

The ideal site architecture is geared toward the buyer journey, and the main landing experience is based on the first step in a buyer journey. Let's continue our example of Janet the CMO considering a solution for her company's big data needs.

The home page for your big data microsite should define what you mean by "big data" and give Janet an infographic or other easily consumed information that explains big data at the highest level. The main call to action might be a TED-style video with an expert in big data inspiring the audience to consider the importance of using big data as a natural resource for marketing. Below that, perhaps you have three calls to action that point Janet to the next stages in her buyer journey. And that's it.

If you launch a microsite with four pages and a few assets, most of your executives would say, "That's it?" Here you need to stand strong. Build your minimum viable product and then iterate, building in links to other content for Janet's journey as time goes along. Eventually, you will plumb this experience down to the conversion or purchase experience. But you start by staking a claim on an area where you have a right to win—not by delaying even longer to build a more elaborate site. If you build a helpful experience, eventually Google will give you credit for your market position, and you will attain higher rankings; this could take four to six months, even if you do everything right. By then, you'll have optimized all the low-hanging fruit and built a user experience that works for the likes of Janet.

Building Quality Content

Once Janet lands on your page from the search engine results, what kind of content experience do you give her? You must actually answer two questions:

- What is quality web content?
- How do you create quality web content?

What Is Quality Web Content?

Ask 10 content strategists at a Confab—the leading content strategy conferences—what quality content is, and you will likely get 10 different answers. Quality is highly subjective, but there are some hallmarks to quality content that most everyone can agree on:

- *Quality content is relevant.* James wrote a whole book about this (*Audience, Relevance, and Search: Targeting Web Audiences with Relevant Content*), so let that serve as the definitive guide. For now, a good proxy for relevance is whether content meets the needs of the user at the time—which is the same thing Google is trying to do. So, if Google is finding your content, perhaps that is the only data point required.

- *Quality content is easily scannable.* How do you demonstrate to web audiences that their content is relevant to them? Provide visual cues that they pick up at a glance—without thinking. If you make it too difficult to determine whether content is relevant to them, they will jump to the conclusion that the content is irrelevant and bounce off your page. When they do, they will likely find a competitor who provides the content they need.

- *Quality content is readable.* Once they determine that the content is relevant, users are willing to think and read. But they will abandon your page if you make reading too difficult. You need to use plain language to communicate with them without forcing them to understand your jargon, buzzwords, or hyperbole. Most importantly, you need to use their language. Making content more readable to your audience is another benefit of using keyword research early and often in content planning and development.

- *Quality content is shareable.* We've talked about shareable content throughout this book, so you shouldn't be surprised that we think quality content has this characteristic. Another way of thinking about it is that you will know that your content is high quality when you see that it is being shared often.

- *Quality content is concise.* Web users are extremely time challenged and impatient. They don't typically go for storytelling or any longer-form content, at least not on the pages themselves. Perhaps assets served from pages—case studies or short white papers—can be longer form. But pure web content needs to be minimalistic.

- *Quality content is credible.* The biggest problem with most marketing content is that it reads like ad copy. Ad copy is typically full of hyperbolic words like "best of breed" without substantiation. The old adage from journalism "show, don't tell" provides guidance here.

- *Quality content uses data.* Unlike ad copy, quality marketing content backs up claims with data—benchmarks, third-party research, and other proof points.

- *Quality content is empathetic.* A corollary to "show, don't tell" is "advise, don't sell." A lot of marketing content employs the hard sell rather than helping buyers come to their own conclusions. Selling stuff before the audience is ready to buy often pushes them away for good.

- *Quality content is clean.* Typos and other mechanical issues degrade user trust. This might seem obvious, but we do see clients try to skimp on editing. They think that the informality of blogs and other native digital content allows for a relaxation of style and usage cleanliness. It doesn't. In an A/B test on ibm.com, edited content got 30% more conversions than unedited content across a wide corpus of information.

It's perhaps this last point that is most important. All of these guidelines are thought to be good ideas, and you can test each one in your situation—just as IBM did. Use these ideas as a starting point but use data to test your assumptions on a regular basis so that your content truly is better in your particular situation with your own customers.

How Do You Create Quality Web Content?

You might know what quality web content looks like when you see it but have no idea how to create it. Investing in writing and editing personnel is the only way to improve your content quality—and it costs less today than ever before. In the move from print to digital, tens of thousands of journalists are unemployed or underemployed. Find them and hire them. They make excellent web content specialists.

When you hire your team, trust them to create the highest-quality content; don't micromanage them. Empower them with tools that check writing errors—including ones that help you standardize on organizational style, usage, and terminology. Don't think of it as automating editing. Think of it as a way of taking the niggling details out of the editing process so that writers and editors can focus on creating quality content.

WRITING SCANNABLE CONTENT

Web visitors don't read pages before scanning them. As it turns out, it is fairly easy to write web content with scanning in mind. Here are some tips:

- *Title.* The title tag needs to contain the keywords—not because the user scans the bar at the top of the browser but because searchers click links in search results that contain their keywords.

- *Main heading (h1).* The main heading is the first place the user scans when she lands on the page, so ensure that the keywords are emphasized there. Beyond putting the keywords in the h1 tag, you need the heading to use active verbs that help scanners understand what the page will help them do.

- *Body copy.* For deep content, body copy needs to be "above the fold," meaning it needs to be one of the first things users see, no matter what device they use. In other words, if you expect readers to scan the copy, don't force them to scroll to see the first few lines of body copy. Bolding one instance of the keyword in the first paragraph is a good way to entice them to scroll for more information.

- *Links.* First of all, the main call to action needs to be above the fold also. The calls to action on the page should tell users what they will get when they download. Don't just say "click here"; rather, say "watch this video on [keyword]."

You have just six seconds to demonstrate that your content is relevant to scanners. You must provide clear visual cues about the relevance of the page to their search keyword or to the task they have in mind—and you need to do it in *text*. Text is important both because Google rarely provides good rankings to pages merely because of strong images and because scanners are looking for *words* to assure them that they are in the right place.

Perhaps most critical is adopting an agile development model. By all means, your content needs to be as clean and clear as you can make it when you publish. But it is always subject to change. Measuring its effectiveness—for example, with A/B testing and heat mapping software—and improving it over time is the way to create quality content. You might lose a few users in the beginning for lack of perfection. But you will gain many more as the content gradually improves over time.

Building Assets for the Buyer Journey

The main point of building a website is not to get people to consume all the quality content on your pages but to get them to take action. Sometimes that action takes the form of a purchase or filling out a contact form, but oftentimes it is merely interacting with a content asset—downloading case studies, white papers, buying guides, and other content assets.

Because assets are always embedded in pages, sometimes you might conflate the two: "That page is a video." But it's more accurate to think that that page contains a video asset. The distinction between assets and pages is important because you can place the same asset on more than one page and because pages can contain multiple assets. Many pages have no separable assets at all—they are merely HTML text and images—and they can cause conversions also, so you might want to think about the meat of that page as an asset, too.

Pages don't help prospects become customers. Assets do. Pages are carriers for those assets.

Effective content marketing is a three-part play:

1. Get your page ranked as highly on Google organic search results as you can, with a quality title, snippet (the piece of text that appears under the title), and schema markup to entice clicks.
2. Build a quality landing page for visitors to determine that the content is relevant to the keyword and worth their time.
3. Serve a high-quality asset that is appropriate to the visitor's state in the buyer journey.

It really is that simple. But if any one of these three does not meet expectations, the whole process fails. It's the last point that we want to focus on here—that the asset is appropriate to the visitor's stage of the buyer journey, which is often the hardest step of the three.

Planning your pages and your assets together is the key to success, but many companies fail to do so, making one of two mistakes:

- *Focusing mostly on pages.* This often happens when a company has grown used to delivering their market messages in text and images in the meat of an HTML page and only now is beginning to embed videos or podcasts or other assets. They might focus on the search optimization and landing experience but slap in whatever asset appears to be on topic. This seems to happen to B2C companies most frequently.

- *Focusing mostly on assets.* You'll commonly see this happen when a company has a history of creating assets but is now integrating them into their website. B2B companies tend to suffer from this error, especially with their libraries of case studies and white papers that have been lovingly crafted as standalone documents without enough thought around search optimization and landing experience.

But even if you overcome these problems, you face the problem that many asset types are not equally welcome in every stage of the buyer journey. Podcasts, blogs, and white papers tend to work best at the top of the funnel—when buyers are at the beginning of their journey, learning about their problems and what products exist to solve them. Our B2B marketing tests show that customers whose last interaction with an asset was downloading a white paper rarely make a purchase; purchasers interact with other assets after the white paper before they buy.

On the other hand, case studies tend to work in the middle of the B2B buyer journey, when prospects want to know if the solution they are considering works for other similar companies. Trials and demos tend to work toward the end of the buyer journey—the bottom of the funnel. These are rules of thumb, of course. You should test these tips in your environment—with your data.

Beyond journey-specific asset guidance, each asset type has its own set of considerations. You want to make sure that assets get the search visibility they deserve, regardless of the search visibility of the pages on which they sit. First, there's no rule against serving the same asset from multiple pages. Yes, search engines penalize you if the majority of your page matches a different page, but just embedding the same video on three different pages is fine. Second, you can sometimes get two listings for the same marketing message on the first page in Google if one of them is a simple page and the other is a page containing an asset. Third, assets and simple pages tend to support each other if both rank well in Google.

TO GATE OR NOT TO GATE?

A fiercely debated topic within content marketing, especially B2B content marketing, is whether to *gate* your most valuable content. *Gating* refers to the practice of placing a registration or other contact form in front of a visitor who wants to see your content—often a white paper or a case study. Some marketers swear that gating is necessary because unless you gather contact information, you can't actually follow up to make a sale—and they can show you the numbers to prove that gating works because they have proof that following up does result in sales.

Other marketers, including your esteemed authors, disagree with the idea that a marketer should offer up the juiciest content only to those who "pay" for it with some contact information.

We've heard the wrongheaded assertion that marketers need to challenge people so that your competitors won't see that valuable content, but that never works because your competitors are always much more diligent about seeing your "secrets" than your customers are. Your customers actually give up rather easily, which is the first problem with gating content. Yes, it qualifies prospects, but maybe not according to their propensity to buy; it's more about how much irritation and loss of privacy they will put up with to see your crown jewel content.

But intelligent marketers disagree on the question of gating because their sales process depends on continually sending in leads from marketing, so they insist on gating content to gather those leads. We have three reasons we think this doesn't makes sense:

- *Your content doesn't get found.* When it is behind a gate, that content can't be indexed by the search spiders and will never be shown in the search results. If the content is as good as you think it is, why hide it from all that search traffic?

- *Your content doesn't get shared.* Most content owners won't link to content behind a gate because it is an annoying user experience that they won't subject their readers to. And it likewise won't be shared in social. These are two more big sources of traffic that you are missing out on. If you miss out on enough extra traffic, you'd need to get a very high conversion rate on those leads for gating to work out to more conversions.

- *Your sales force gets a lot of bum leads to run down.* Many customers have special "dead letter office" email addresses that they use only to look at gated content, but some poor soul in sales has to follow up and follow up until finally declaring the lead dead—a complete waste of time. The alternative—taking down the gate and putting up a contact form for those who really *want* to be contacted—results in a solid set of leads that are a pleasure to pursue and that convert at much higher rates. Less time for the sales force and higher conversions…seems like a good idea.

But don't just listen to us. We have given you our opinion. But opinions are like necks: Everybody has one. Instead, you can easily answer this question with data because it is testable. If you've got all your content behind gates, take down some of the gates and watch your conversion rate. It might take a few months for Google to discover your content and start sending people there, but it will happen. Once that happens, more readers will share the content. And some people will ask to be contacted. Give your test a good long run—maybe six months—and make sure to optimize your content for search, put up social sharing buttons, and track the leads through to actual sales.

If sales go up, take down all the gates. If not, put things back as they were. Your customers can tell you what works better if you give them a choice. Every time we've gotten a client to test, the walls have all come down. But try it yourself and see. We've tested it only a few times, and that isn't exactly overwhelming evidence. But you don't care about overwhelming evidence. What you care about is what will work better for you. That is what your data will tell you.

Videos

Of all of the types of assets you can choose from, it's hard to go wrong with videos. Videos work for both B2B and B2C marketers, and while they can directly show off your product, they can also feature someone speaking about almost any subject. Perhaps best of all, the advent of the smart phone means that videos work wonderfully on any device. Moreover, videos are so important that they have their own search engine—YouTube.

If your budget allows you to concentrate on just one type of asset, videos would be the right type for most marketers, who should make videos the cornerstone of their content strategy.

Fitting with our theme in this chapter, videos also have another remarkable quality: They can be appropriate at just about any step in the buyer journey. From TED-style talks at the start of the journey to gorpy how-to videos for the postpurchase phases of the customer relationship, lots of different kinds of videos can be effective.

You might get hung up on having high-production values. Don't. Some of the best-performing videos on YouTube are low-fi how-to videos or vlogs from self-made celebrities who record themselves in their grungy offices with smart phones. That's not the right image for every brand, but it might be worth testing before you dismiss it out of hand; it certainly would be a lot cheaper than trying to look like a professional broadcast network.

If you're convinced of the importance of videos, you'll want to know how to ensure that your videos are found by your intended audience. As we said, videos are an unusual asset type in that they have their own search engine. If you want your videos to be findable, you must publish them on YouTube; because YouTube does not crawl the web looking for video content, merely publishing videos on your own site will hide them from search. So upload your videos to YouTube and embed them on your web pages.

Like many other graphics-intensive assets, videos require a lot of text to clue the search engines into their subject; search engines don't watch and understand videos yet. Make sure that the YouTube page where you upload your video contains a long description of the video's content—even a transcript, if that seems appropriate. You should include the keywords you expect people to search for to locate your video, just as you would do for any other kind of content.

Once your video is found, and viewed, the next step to focus on is getting viewers to click through to your website to continue the buyer journey. YouTube refers to these as Call to Action overlays, and you'll pay for each click to your site, but this is the most friction-free way to convert YouTube traffic into visitors to your website. You might also be able to use a free alternative for clicks to your site, called video annotations. Annotations are best used as persistent calls to action at the bottom of the video. When users click them, they should land on content that represents their next logical step in the buyer journey.

To know how well your video is performing, use measurements to count how often it is viewed and how often viewers click through to your site. You can also measure behavior that can be difficult to measure in other types of content assets. For example, the average viewing time metric can help you determine which videos are working and which are not in terms of length. High abandonment rates early in the video might also mean it just doesn't deliver on its promise.

Perhaps an obvious point for some is that video is more effective if you spread out your publishing schedule rather than dump a large batch on You-Tube at once. Unfortunately, while no one would think to publish a month's worth of blog posts in a single day, we've seen cases where a brand commissions an agency to produce a batch of videos by a certain deadline, and the whole pile is uploaded at the eleventh hour. This leads to the odd situation of YouTube channels having 20 videos loaded about every six weeks, with nothing in between. Shoot for publishing a new video about every other day in every active channel so that you publish at the rate your audience can comfortably consume. No one is waiting with anticipation to "binge watch" your marketing content.

Blogs

Blogs are one of the oldest types of content assets, and one of the most popularly used forms for marketers. But despite the perennial popularity of blogs—in many ways replacing periodical magazines and newspapers from the print world—many brand marketers have failed to capitalize on this popularity and have created blogs with all the charm of a press release or an old company newspaper.

Blogs can effectively foster community on your site if you enable comments and do the appropriate outreach and promotion. But they are not often done well at the corporate level. The best blogs encourage an internal community of experts to regularly blog about a topic in which the company has a right to win by virtue of their expertise. This community connects with peer influencers outside the walls of the blog, encouraging them to join the community and follow or comment on the blog. If you run your blogs this way, you won't need to worry about search visibility because you will be gaining subdomain authority with each new blog post. The bylines of these bloggers gain value over time as the community gains new followers and subscribers.

In our experience, corporate blogs are rarely run this way. They tend to turn into venues for occasional ghost-written posts by executives. The ghost writers commonly are media relations professionals who write the blog posts like press releases, carefully crafting each line to avoid any risk of overstatement or controversy. Not only do all the executives have the same voice (the corporate voice), they never write anything that might incite comment. Blogs like this are just glorified PR, and they will not gain any subdomain authority or search visibility. Because they are occasional, the executive bylines mean little to the community at large.

If instead a blog focuses on thought leadership—what's new and interesting in your industry, new uses for products or services, and especially problems that your offerings solve—you'll find that it captures significant traffic at the top of the funnel and that it spurs the discussion needed to get an entire community to promote your content.

Setting up a winning blog site is definitely worth the time and effort. Most experts are not writers by trade, so they will need some sort of boot camp writing training followed by a lot of regular editorial guidance. This is quite labor intensive, but don't be too concerned with the cost because the benefits can hardly be overstated. If your top pages have blogs associated with them, you can curate the best posts on your pages and always have fresh insights from which to draw for your audience.

Podcasts

Podcasts offer a handy way for some of your audience members to consume content while they attend to other matters, such as commuting or working out. As such, they have some value. But expecting your audience to get a lot out of an audio file with half their attention might be a bit optimistic. So we recommend keeping podcasts light and not too taxing. Podcasts tend to be much more effective at the top of the funnel than to convey more detailed information.

Some companies have corporate evangelists who are celebrities in their own right. Podcasts by these folks can gain a lot of reach, especially if they are regularly recorded—like a weekly address. Still, unless you have special audiences who look for them, we don't recommend a heavy use of podcasts because it is difficult to continue the buyer journey at your website from a podcast.

If you do find that podcasts are part of *your* audience's regular media consumption, make them findable. First, like videos, they need text wrappers for Google and others to properly index and rank them in their search results. Also, make sure the name of the podcaster is prominently displayed in your text. The authority of the podcaster is a key signal for Google.

Finally, use well-worn techniques from radio and television to try to get listeners to take the next step. Make sure that you provide an easy-to-remember and easy-to-spell URL that you repeat several times so that the audience can come to your site when they have the chance. While it's great to reach someone during their workout, don't expect them to be jumping to your website then. Emulate radio commercials designed to imprint a brand name in your head while you are driving so that you will take action after you reach your destination.

White Papers

White papers are a longstanding part of B2B marketing—and have some appeal in B2C also—but their long-form approach can sometimes seem dated for contemporary readers. White papers tend to lack audience focus; they can be too technical for executives and too rudimentary for the line-of-business professionals. They often don't play well on mobile devices because of their size and scale. They force readers to consume more information than needed to answer their questions. And they are difficult to update and maintain, so they tend to get out of date before they are taken down.

Despite these drawbacks, there is still a place for white papers, and when they are done well, they can be helpful, especially in the early stages of the buyer journey. We recommend limiting their use to specific buyers, such as technical professionals. We also recommend making sure they provide the detail needed to answer these professionals' questions. So you have to get experts involved in writing and reviewing them. Finally, we recommend keeping them as short and tightly focused as possible. Ask a common audience question in the heading and answer it in the body, with the kind of detail needed to develop the confidence of your more technical audiences.

If companies all followed these recommendations, most of them would produce a fraction of the white papers they do. And that's okay. They can transfer the resources devoted to building white papers to building videos or blogs.

If you do produce white papers in PDF format, make sure to include the document properties before posting to your website. If you've added the appropriate keywords in the document properties metadata fields, your white paper has a chance to rank well in search. If these fields are not filled out, there is no chance. It's just that simple.

Case Studies

Storytelling has been the hot topic across content marketing for the past few years, with trendy websites taking a more literary approach. Color us skeptical on this approach because the web medium itself is literal, favoring plain language over metaphor. But there is one place where storytelling is required: the case study.

Case studies are nothing new. They have been a staple of vertical publications for decades, especially those oriented toward technology. The tech press, from *Computerworld* and *Infoworld* to *Wired* and *ZDnet*, relies heavily on this content type to fill its magazines and websites. The reason is simple: Their readers like them. People making buying decisions read the case studies to compare the companies profiled in those stories with their own. Research has shown case studies to be the most persuasive content that a company can provide about its offerings. This makes sense because case studies are similar to positive user reviews: They show that what the company is selling works for real-life customers.

The most effective case studies are assets in the traditional sense but are digital first. This means that they are built in HTML and served as clickable assets on a page, perhaps with a thumbnail image and a bit of teaser text. At the end of the case study, you can add calls to action for the next logical phases of the buyer journey, such as a trial or demo. It is also important to tag case studies by the company profiled and the industry it occupies (using Schema.org markup). This will help both readers and bots decide whether a particular case study is relevant to them.

Case studies can be used at any point in the buyer journey but tend to be most effective in the middle or at the end. At the beginning of the journey, customers are still trying to understand their problem and the range of solutions. Case studies are most effective in persuading a prospect that *your* solution to their problem is the best one, which happens later in the buying process.

Demos

Once a buyer is convinced that a solution could work for her, she will want to know *how* it works. This is where demo content comes in. Some types of digital products, such as software, movies, music, or ebooks, can be demonstrated or sampled directly, but many products can be shown off with a video demonstration. Not all offerings benefit from demonstrations—car insurance doesn't seem like a good candidate—but even these services might benefit from an expert talking about the process.

Toy retailer Step2 faces the problem that retailers stock only a few of its large-scale toys (think kid-size play houses), so they must somehow show the value of their products online to sell what retailers won't give floor space for. They focused on a series of video demonstrations that help consumers visualize their child playing with their toys, using simple touches such as depicting an average-sized mom in each video to help consumers understand the true size of each toy. Some toys include electronic components such as working doorbells for the play houses, so showing those off in the demo also shows the value of the product—and at $140 for an average product, Step2 needs to show the value. With a catalog of more than 100 videos, Step2 has seen that video viewers are 174% more likely to convert than non-viewers.

There's no substitute for demonstrating an experience. For example, before James recently bought a guitar, he watched videos of several artists playing one particular class of guitars. These demonstrations convinced him to buy one particular make and model within that class. In this case, the demos weren't even made by the manufacturer (Martin). Martin *fans* produced the videos.

And so it goes with demo content. Fans and third-party vendors regularly review products in demo form and publish them to YouTube. If you can find and curate this content for the product pages at the bottom of the funnel, you will get conversions. Demos and their cousin, full-fledged product trials, occur later in the buyer journey and often are the trigger for a sale.

Promoting Content

You've probably noticed that we emphasize using search marketing techniques to promote your content marketing assets—and that we emphasize the quality of those assets to get people to share them in social media. But there is still a place for directly promoting content to influencers and aggregators—just not always using the same techniques as old-fashioned public relations.

In the old days, PR folks built press releases that included the URLs for the pages in the content of the releases. This still needs to be done, but its effectiveness is waning—for a couple reasons:

- Google has cracked down on intentional link building where it borders on manipulation. Experts now advise publishers not to artificially orchestrate links using link-building campaigns that go after links more for their value to search marketing than the value of the links themselves. Now understand, you still need to put links in press releases. And as long as you do, you might as well use the most effective URLs and anchor text (the text you click when you link to something). But avoid *loading* press releases with link lists. And stop doing typical media relations link-building activities, such as sponsored content and guest blogs that serve to promote the URLs and little else. When you set out to manipulate, you're more likely to hurt your search marketing than help it.

- Press releases are becoming less effective as the media evolves toward a model where key influencers self-publish through blogs outside mainstream media. Unlike traditional media, individual influencers don't respond well to press releases. Again, as long as you are creating press releases, do them right. But start shifting your focus toward other ways of promoting your content that are more likely to actually influence the influencers.

The best way to promote your content is to enable your site visitors to easily share your assets from your pages. Few users share typical web pages. But they will share videos or blogs or even white papers if the assets are especially compelling. Most of our clients struggle to encourage sharing, however, because it is difficult to code your pages with the right interactivity to help users share. We will discuss this in more depth in the next chapter. For now, just know that designing for shareability is worth the investment.

Don't overlook coaxing your employees to share your content but also don't just ask every employee to share the same stuff; it may seem easy, but it is also remarkably similar to email spam. Instead, try these ideas:

- *Train employees as brand ambassadors.* Encourage your employees to be active in social media to support your marketing but educate them on *how* to do this. The interactions have to fit your brand. Some employees might be too informal in their interactions if you are reaching other corporate clients. Don't hawk products like a used car salesman unless you are actually selling used cars. If your employees act in social media the way you'd want them to act in person, you are probably doing it right.

- *Focus your attention on your most influential employees.* Try to limit sharing to your top influencer employees who already have a lot of friends and followers. A common trap is to encourage a lot of sharing by your employees only to find them overhyping everything, which damages the brand. It is better to have a few designated brand ambassadors write the tweets and other posts and to let the rambunctious masses re-tweet them. Even then, it would be better for them to add their own spin so that your employees are not just mindlessly re-tweeting the same things, but you should focus your training, attention, and mentoring on the employees who are building a genuine following.

- *Help them share the right links.* Left to their own devices, your employees might share a portal URL rather than a genuine asset URL. If you work with a URL-shortening vendor, you can manage the URLs your ambassadors promote in their posts. Don't assume that they know the best content or the best URL; help them share the best stuff.

The reason social sharing—typically an outbound marketing topic—is also a helpful inbound tactic is that it helps you organically promote the links on your pages externally. The shares themselves might not garner much link equity in Google, but the promoted links will be picked up by the external influencers who have the credibility to enhance your credibility quickly.

Wrapping Up: Sound Strategy Is the Key to Content Marketing

Content strategy is the key to content marketing. Without a solid content strategy, content marketing just leads to content shock, overwhelming your audience with a confusing mix of competing messages that your various teams publish *en masse*. In this chapter, we have presented a sustainable outside-in content strategy, focusing on the highest-value keywords for which your company has a right to win—that is, where your company differentiates itself from your competitors. Your strategy should build content from the top down, prioritized by keyword demand, including not just web pages but content assets tuned to the buyer journey. If you build relevant pages containing quality assets, you will achieve the search visibility you deserve and help your target personas complete their buyer journeys. The more users complete their buyer journeys, the more leads and sales your site will drive.

We wrap up this book with our next chapter, Chapter 6, which looks at how user experience and design affect content marketing.

KRISTINA HALVORSON, ON THE ERROR OF MANDATING CONTENT MARKETING

Kristina Halvorson is the author of the book Content Strategy for the Web, *with Melissa Rach, and the founder and CEO of Brain Traffic, a Minneapolis-based content strategy consultancy. She is also founder of Confab Events, which puts on several content strategy conferences a year. A frequent speaker at conferences around the world, Kristina is widely recognized as a leading expert in the content strategy discipline.*

Tell us a little bit about how you got into content strategy, who your influencers are, and what you're most proud of in your career.

I started as a web copywriter in the late '90s. In working with both agencies and in-house content teams, I found that my work was always the last thing they did before going live. I noticed over and over again that no one had been thinking strategically about content when they planned or built web pages. There were a lot of boxes, a lot of content requirements, but no real thought given to content purpose, let alone what would happen to the content after it was published. Who was going to take care of it? So I started inserting myself into the planning process. I started making sure that the stakeholders were asking the right questions as often and as soon as possible. Then, in 2008—by which point I'd hired staff—we formally "branded" our work as content strategy. We were all craving information about content strategy at that time. There just wasn't a lot out there. The only authorities I could really find were Ann Rockley, Gerry McGovern, and Rachel Lovinger. So I mined LinkedIn and Twitter for anyone doing this kind of work. While there weren't many people calling themselves content strategists at the time, many of us like-minded "content enthusiasts" started regularly connecting, and before we knew it, there was a bona fide content strategy community active on social media and (soon) at local meetups. I published *Content Strategy for the Web* in 2009, and I later updated it with Melissa Rach (partner, Dialog Studios). Since then, I've done a lot of writing and speaking about content strategy, which continues to be really gratifying.

As the discipline of content strategy has grown and evolved, how has that shaped your business, Brain Traffic?

For many years, 100% of the work we did is what I now call "content strategy for UX design." It largely focused on the editorial and structural aspects of content. We helped companies decide what to create, how to shape it, when to introduce it in the user journey, and so on. I'd say that now that work comprises about 50% of our projects. The other 50% is really working at a very strategic level with enterprises about where they're going to focus their content efforts, not just with content products but also with content process and people. I do a lot of work with leadership to help articulate business goals and success metrics in relation to content initiatives, then help them prioritize those initiatives based on where they are in the "content maturity model." Are they still in a reactive publishing mode? Have they built the appropriate infrastructure? What kind of shape is their current content in? I will say that, oftentimes, once that work is completed, those companies will hire Brain Traffic to execute that strategy, which is always fun—seeing a project through implementation is very satisfying.

In summary, our business services have evolved from just being about content substance and structure to also encompassing workflow and governance. And I'm really enjoying the consulting work I'm doing—it's almost more management consulting, helping leaders communicate expected outcomes and accountability to their content teams so everyone's on the same page about what content strategy needs to accomplish.

My dad recently said, "So, you're getting paid to give people your opinion? That's the perfect job for you." For what it's worth, having nearly 20 years of experience with messy content problems has in fact shaped some of my (pretty strong) opinions—so, yeah, maybe he's right!

You have been an outspoken critic of content marketing. What is the primary reason for this criticism?

Companies choose content marketing as a strategy without doing the due diligence of setting meaningful business goals, assessing their current content ecosystem, and analyzing challenges and opportunities. They just assume it's the right thing to do, without asking, "Why is this the right marketing strategy for us to pursue?" Are there other places content efforts can have a positive impact on their business outcomes and customer satisfaction?

You hear stuff like "If you don't hop on the content marketing bus, your business will get run over" all the time. It drives me crazy.

It's similar to what happened with social media marketing years ago. Everyone had to do it. But once people jumped in, they often couldn't figure out how to tie their efforts to business results. Eventually, many companies started figuring that out and started focusing their efforts on much smarter social media tactics, or shifted to using social media more for customer service. So, similarly, I think the hype around content marketing as a mandate will die down within the next three years, for sure. Eventually, executives will get tired of spending their money on content marketing with no meaningful results.

In the meantime, starting with content marketing as the answer versus an option is proving to be a dangerous trap. I have a lot of angst about it. Companies immediately focus on content creation, which leads to so much waste that has nothing to do with the business objectives. They end up overwhelming the audience with volume rather than focusing on creating the right content, and only what is needed... which sometimes is the boring stuff in the Support section.

So you're saying that content marketing leads to content shock, which creates more problems for the audience than it solves.

It's not to say that I'm against it as a practice; I'm against it as a mandate. It's not necessary, and it can be more harmful to a brand than helpful. Think about how you start your day. Before you even get out of bed, you encounter brands on your pillows, your sheets, your blankets, etc. Before you even get out of bed, you might encounter

20 brands. For how many of those brands do you subscribe to their newsletter? How many of those brands do you follow on Twitter? Why do they feel like they need to publish all this content to provide the kind of brand experience that makes a difference?

When you think of content marketing as a mandate, you begin to manage the whole practice from a set of checklists. "We need a newsletter, a Twitter feed, a corporate blog, etc." They're focused on checklists and quantity and scale rather than business purpose or outcomes. Content marketing is not laddering up to business problems; it's fundamentally founded on the assumption that visibility leads to engagement leads to trust, which is a shaky equation at best.

How about companies that do it well? Do you have any stories to share along these lines?

That's a difficult question to answer. I have yet to see many studies showing positive impact on their business and customer satisfaction (CSAT) from content marketing. It can't just be that we create great content. We can't confuse activity with results. We as an industry can celebrate great content. Kmart had great content about how you could ship things from the store [the Ship My Pants campaign]. Did any of it change buying behavior? No. It created passing attention, which is cheap and fleeting.

So how do we change the conversation toward results rather than volume?

We need to stop using cheap metrics—clicks, shares, time on page—as indicators of success. Content success equals business outcomes and customer satisfaction. That's all there is. And that's what we need to talk about to change the conversation.

6

User Experience: Helping Buyers Make Purchasing Decisions

The five-person web design team for a large corporation nervously shifted in their leather chairs around the way-too-large mahogany table, while waiting for their newly appointed executive to arrive. They had reason to be nervous. Their new executive, three levels up from them, had requested the meeting because she wanted to review the new design system they had been working on for several months, in preparation for the upcoming website redesign for the company.

The new executive walked in, greeted everyone, and sat at the end of the long table. The manager of the design team had prepared for days for this moment, but nothing could have prepared him for what would follow.

The manager launched into his meticulously prepared presentation (designers always have great-looking slides), opening with the mock-up of the website's redesigned home page, which highlighted the new, more muted gray color scheme that was the centerpiece of the new design concept.

"How did you choose these colors?" the executive interjected.

The veteran design manager was accustomed to executives questioning color choices. He believed that all execs fancy themselves as having good taste, and color is the one area of design that they can discuss without risking looking foolish. He confidently shifted to one of his backup slides, prepared for just this question, showing how gray tones were trendy in the design community and that two other tony corporations with the same type of clientele had recently shifted to similar color schemes.

"But what else did you test?" the executive pressed on. "How can you be sure that this change will improve our sales? I need to be confident of that before we can make this change to our entire global website."

To describe the resulting look on the face of the design manager as resembling "a deer in the headlights" is unfair to all those deer who appear far more confident when facing down a truck.

As the conversation continued, it was clear that not only was there no plan to limit the downside risks of this radical visual change to the entire website, but no one even knew what the compelling reason was to make any change at all. There was no evidence that the current website had any visual problem, except that this company always conducted a redesign every three years, so they felt that the website looked "dated."

Soon, the massive redesign project was canceled, replaced by a long series of tests in small-market countries of several new designs—along with a wave of other user experience enhancements that were based on specific data showing where customers were having difficulty. Two years later the company redesigned its global website on the basis of the results of these tests, but with virtually the original color scheme they started with—and delivered a marked increase in sales.

This executive transformed the way her teams worked to a new process for improving user experience—one that actually puts the user at the center of the process. In this chapter, we'll unpack this process step by step:

- Finding the problems
- Fixing the problems
- Propagating the fixes

We can use data to find problems, experiment with fixes on a small scale until something is working, and then reuse those ideas to solve similar problems across a site. But before we launch into the new process, we want to review the first principles of user experience (UX).

THE THREE MOST COMMON MISTAKES IN UX WORK

User experience done well is a goal of every company; no one sets out to do it wrong. But the road to bad UX is paved with good intentions, and here are the three pitfalls we most often see:

- *UX is, above all, art.* Designers are artists at their core—which is good. They create beautiful experiences that make a positive impression. But they can't make the beauty of the art the highest goal of what they do. UX teams need to be driven first and foremost by an empathy for the user—a need to make the experience pleasant and welcoming for a person—rather than art for art's sake.

- *It's not ready until it is perfect.* Sometimes designers fall into this trap, but more frequently it is managers and executives who are so wary of being criticized for the slightest flaw that they allow the perfect to drive out the good. A website is not a book or a painting; it can always be changed again tomorrow.

- *I know better than my customers.* When designers have a lot of personal pride invested in their creations, they are reluctant to accept data to the contrary—and UX generates increasing amounts of data each year to show whether experiences are working for actual customers. Data-driven UX, not a designer's opinion, must drive decisions.

The job of the UX designer is as much about serving as an advocate for the user as it is about supporting the central practices at the core of the profession (design, information architecture, usability, accessibility, etc.). In our experience, the most effective way to do this is to let the results speak for themselves. If your web analytics measure business results, resistance becomes counterproductive to the goals of the organization. This principle applies to everyone responsible for a website, including UX designers.

User Experience Basics

User experience is the original outside-in marketing practice because the best UX design comes from the user's perspective. This means learning users' needs and being laser-focused on serving them in the simplest, most elegant way.

UX combines everything that goes into the interaction with your online customer. (Your company might include offline customer experience, too, but that's not our area of expertise.) We're admittedly lumping arguably separate practices such as *information architecture* and *web design* into user experience because we believe that they should all be done using the same orchestrated process.

UX is a great way to end this book because it is a field increasingly awash in data. In Figure 6-1, we illustrate a typical user scenario, showing how it can end well (or badly) for the company. You can imagine how much data can be collected along the way to reveal both ultimate success and failure as well as the seeds of those outcomes.

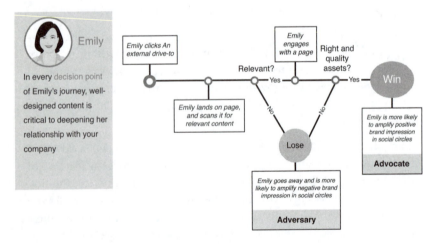

Figure 6-1   The basic user flow of content marketing.

This simple diagram describes the central use case of outside-in content marketing. Emily starts with some type of "drive-to-web" stimulus, such as clicking on a search result. When Emily lands on your page, she spends (on average) six seconds deciding whether your content is relevant to the stimulus that brought her there. In the case of search, she scans the page for visual cues that make the page relevant, such as finding her keywords in the headings, body copy, and pull quotes. If your experience doesn't clearly and quickly demonstrate relevance, she will go somewhere else, or she will "pogo stick" back to the search results. Emily's first scan is as automatic as breathing—she's not consciously thinking. (That's why one of our favorite books on designing good user experiences is *Don't Make Me Think* by Stephen Krug.)

Once she determines that the page is relevant, she will start reading, scrolling, and clicking. When she clicks the call to action for the ultimate content asset you provide—video, podcast, case study—it needs to deliver on the promise of the page. The whole purpose of the page is to convince Emily that it has what she is looking for. She is looking for an asset that will answer the question implicit in her query. The more assets you deliver, the less likely she will find the right one. So keep it simple, with no more than three assets to a page.

As simple as this diagram might appear, it is a radical concept for many digital marketing organizations. Why? Because they are often more focused on their own content marketing goals than on user goals. Their designs are often unsuccessful because they're not focused on meeting user goals but on the goals of their organizations. For example, they're focused on getting registrations for a particular asset when that is not the asset users are looking for.

In our experience, designs that are focused on user goals are easy to spot. They all have three key features:

- *Simple.* A page should have a single purpose. If it does, it should be easy to serve that purpose in the simplest way. Teams that struggle to create simple designs typically start with pages that are trying to do too much. Inventions like carousels and other dynamic designs signal that you should create multiple experiences rather than trying to serve multiple purposes with one experience. So keep it simple. Use keyword data to deliver the right asset, which will gain trust and lead to deeper engagement with your content and your offerings.

- *Clean.* Pages should not be cluttered with irrelevant graphics or stock photos. Graphics should serve a purpose—not merely to break up gray text but to help visitors determine at a glance that the page is relevant and to take relevant action. You should, however, have a featured image that makes the page more attractive when shared in social media.

- *Textual.* Many designers we have worked with have said that "visitors don't read on the web, so they're not looking for text." First of all, users *do* scan the text for words that are relevant to the search keywords that led them to the page. Second, when users determine that the page is relevant, they *do* read text—as long as it helps them answer their questions or solve their problems.

Some studies (e.g., Jakob Nielsen's seminal study, "Why Web Users Scan Instead of Reading") that were conducted to prove that users don't read on the web had two crucial flaws: They used designs that made reading difficult and text that gave users little incentive to read. Still, these studies are often cited (many years later) in web design training and literature. Hence, we need to let go of the idea that users do not read web pages.

The primary reason for text on a page is to help the user understand the context. They are coming to your unfamiliar design from the familiarity of search results pages. They are often dropping into the middle of your experience without having experienced the carefully crafted introductory pages. They need to know that the page is worth their time. Text is what many people use to determine that. Even in the case of a page that contains non-text assets, the first decision users face when they land on your page is whether it is worth their time to consume the asset (e.g., play a video, listen to a podcast). At minimum, the text needs to persuade them to.

With that background, we are now ready to tackle the three parts of the UX improvement process, starting with how we actually find the problems in the UX.

Finding the Problems

The easiest way to identify experiences that need to be upgraded is to use data. You must use several data points to identify problems with your UX because Emily can get frustrated at any point in her journey. Identifying her frustrations and eliminating them is the point of UX upgrades.

The major indicators of UX bottlenecks are content with:

- High bounce rates
- Low engagement rates
- Low conversion rates
- Low advocacy rates

Let's look at each one in turn.

High Bounce Rates

Recall that a *bounce* is registered each time someone comes to your page but then immediately abandons your site. Good bounce rates are in the 30% range. Bad bounce rates are in the 80% range. If you put all your top-ranking pages on a chart and sort them by bounce rate, the resulting spreadsheet can serve as a backlog of pages to upgrade.

Content marketing can include many ways for visitors to discover your content, but we'll concentrate on search because it is the most important. If your page has good search visibility and you get decent click numbers, but visitors bounce at a high rate, it's a good indication that you are not doing enough to demonstrate that the page is relevant to Emily's search keyword. If your bounce rates are over 50%, the page needs work. When a page has high bounce rates, you're forcing users like Emily to work too hard to understand the relevance of the page to the search query they entered into Google.

Users scan pages listed in Google's search results before deciding which pages are worth their time and attention. Users do this automatically, like breathing. They don't commit to reading, scrolling, or clicking until this automatic process takes place. So the goal of search-friendly UX is to demonstrate relevance without making users think. And this needs to be done for all kinds of devices—tablets, PCs, and especially phones.

The simple fix is to make sure that the main heading and the first part of the body copy are the first things users see, and they both need to have the keyword in a place where the scanning eye can recognize it. It goes without saying that this needs to be above the "fold"—meaning the first pane of content that a user sees, regardless of the device.

Low Engagement Rates

Engagement is perhaps the fuzziest kind of measurement our clients use—not because you can't define it precisely and measure it scientifically, but because people tend to define it in many different ways. If different people define it differently in the same marketing organization, they could be failing to communicate about the relative effectiveness of their content marketing. So the most important thing is to standardize on a definition that works for your organization and stick with it.

All definitions of engagement start with the absence of bounce. If someone bounces, they are, by definition, *not* engaging with the page. But if they don't bounce, what do they do? Typically, they read, scroll, and click, in that order. The best engagement metrics include these three elements.

The main problem with including these three elements is that they are not all easy to measure. Reading, in particular, is almost impossible to measure. A proxy for reading that is often used is the *time on page* metric. But time on page is a really noisy number for today's browsers and devices. Users can start to read something, get a phone call, check their email, and then return to the article. There is no way of knowing that they were actually reading the whole time they were on the page.

Scrolling is easier to measure. You can use *heat mapping software*, which measures how users move their mice, where they click, and the degree to which they scroll. Heat mapping software can even help you measure reading if you have body copy that users have to scroll to complete. We do not recommend forcing users to scroll in order to read at least some of the body copy, but if they can get the essentials without scrolling and then they scroll for more detailed information, it is a good indicator that they are reading the content. On mobile devices, designers are forced to give users a taste of what's to come, so scrolling is an even better indicator of reading.

If you see low scrolling or clicking rates for those who do not bounce, it is an indicator that the content is not compelling. It might be relevant, but perhaps it is redundant or otherwise lacking in presentation. One common mistake writers make is to write for the web as though they are writing for print. Scanning is common to both print and the web. But print readers tend to read more uninterrupted text. On the web, readers tend to prefer shorter sentences, shorter paragraphs, more bullets—smaller chunks of information, called "snackable" text.

If your scrolling and clicking rates are low, try removing needless words, breaking down longer sentences into shorter ones, creating bulleted lists, and so on. Your heat mapping software will tell you where you need to try these things.

The other typical root cause of poor engagement is a lack of compelling images or calls to action. Using infographics is a particularly good way to increase engagement rates because they combine snackable text with explanatory images in much more compelling ways than the typical stock photos. Videos are another form of particularly compelling calls to action. They don't force a long commitment but rather break up the information task into multimedia experiences.

The crux of engagement is giving users what they need to complete their information task. If you do it in an accessible, clean, and clear way, they will stay on your page and scroll for more. If you overwhelm them with too much information that does not help them with the particular information task implicit in their keyword, you will lose them before you are able to convert them. Each abandonment experience might create a potential adversary, who might just amplify the negative experiences in social circles. The stakes are high to create experiences your target audiences want to engage with.

Low Conversion Rates

For each user experience, an asset must enable the user to take a deeper dive into the content. Perhaps it's a client case study or a demo video or even a white paper. When users click these experiences, marketers like to call it a *conversion*. Conversions are so important to marketers that they will do everything they can to capture the users who convert on these experiences, even to the point of forcing users to fill out long surveys that require entry of personal information.

Whether or not it is a good experience to gate content in this way (Hint: It's often not.), enticing the user to opt into experiences and capturing some of their user information is a definitional aspect of conversion. It demonstrates a level of commitment that implies that the user is ready to be contacted. It is rightly a critical goal of content marketing.

But marketers who do not give users an equal-value exchange for the time and effort it takes to fill out a form are thwarting their own efforts. The central problem is, as a user, how do I know that the content I am forced to register for will give me equal value for my time and attention? That uncertainty causes a lot of abandonment. When you see a lot of abandonment, your first response should be to take the registration form out of the equation.

How then do you measure conversion if you don't have a registration form in front of your content? More importantly, how can you get the business results you need if you don't get names and contact information from your users? There is a very simple answer: Launch a registration form at the end of the asset. If they think the content is worth giving their personal information after they have consumed it, this is a vote of confidence for the content. Also, it is a better test of not only the content itself but the placement of the asset in the buyer's journey. If they have consumed the content and they still don't want to give you their personal information, they're not ready to become your client. They need more information to get to the point of conversion. In that case, it's better not to waste the time of your sales force in contacting them.

This is what testing conversion rates is all about: where and when to present your best content to the audience so that they willingly accept the terms and conditions of a client relationship. If an asset is getting a lot of clicks but the form at the end is typically left blank, take the form away and simply give users a way to dive deeper into other assets, which in turn could have registration forms at the end.

Understand that merely counting conversions might not make sense, especially with multistop buying cycles that take time to unfold. The best thing that content in the first step of your process can do is to get the visitor to the *next* step, so it makes no sense to test top-of-funnel content against conversions. Treating the transition from step 1 to step 2 as a "microconversion" gives you a better way to test the content from step 1.

If you don't get conversions, you should at least tag and track the user so that you can remarket to her later. Tagging and tracking technology places a cookie on the user's device, which is like a digital fingerprint that cues into the user's behavior without gathering any personally identifiable information. When the same user returns, you can offer her another asset that is the next logical step in her journey, based on the data you have collected about typical client journeys.

Another way to optimize conversion is to test different assets. For example, videos work particularly well in the early steps of client journeys because they can be coded with annotations to drive clicks to the next logical step. If you use videos later in the journey (perhaps as how-to demos), you can offer an annotation at the end that loads a registration form or a purchase experience. There's no end to the variables you can test in order to improve your conversion experiences.

Low Advocacy Rates

Advocacy is difficult, but not impossible, to measure. We recommend using social sharing as a proxy for advocacy. If Emily shares your content in her social circles, that's an implicit endorsement of your content and the brand that created it. Measuring social sharing is at least a critical first step in assessing the degree to which your content is generating advocacy.

When measuring the advocacy rate of your content, don't confuse content-fueled advocacy with general brand advocacy. Some companies use social listening to determine whether clients are advocating their brand; they use brand mentions with positive sentiment as a measure of advocacy. This is a perfectly valid thing to measure, but the problem is that it usually does not tie back to any particular content asset, so it is not a helpful measurement for identifying poor UX. In addition, there's no way to prove that any changes you made in your content directly affected the brand advocacy metric gathered through social listening.

Another mistake we often see with measuring content advocacy rates is measuring only the sharing done through the Twitter or Facebook sharing buttons you place on your page. While we strongly advocate the use of such buttons, we know that the great majority of social happens through "dark social"—users sharing by copying and pasting URLs into emails and tweets rather than clicking the nice buttons you gave them.

Whether or not Emily uses your sharing buttons, you can test all kinds of things about the assets she shares: the placement of the assets on the page, the pages from which the assets are served, the calls to action for the assets themselves, etc. Even if you have the best assets in the world, nobody will share them if they fail to scroll down the page to find them, for example. In these ways, UX is a crucial aspect of social interaction, including sharing.

So, by identifying assets with high bounce rates, or low rates of engagement, conversion, and advocacy, you'll put together your first draft of the most likely culprits in compromising your UX. Obviously, the pages with the most views combined with these identifying metrics are the ones to target first. Once you know where the problems are, it's time to fix them.

Fixing the Problems

It might seem daunting to try to fix so many problems, but the beauty of using analytics to identify the problems is that those same analytics give you clues about what is wrong—and they help you test what you've done to prove the improvement.

But how do you start this kind of painstaking process in the first place? In our experience, when you answer that question, you've reached your personal inflection point between success and failure in outside-in marketing. Depending on where you work, you might see it go many different ways:

- You take over a small set of pages on your site that you can change over and over again without asking permission.
- You make friends with the analytics manager, who feeds you proof of all the problem areas of the site that you take to management to get funding for fixes.
- You convince an executive to let you do a pilot aligned with better UX practices.

In each case, the next step is the critical one. You keep working on that problem until you begin to improve the results. As we'll see later, that success allows you to make the case to scale the solution to a larger swath of the website.

Let's start the process of fixing the problems by understanding how to generate ideas.

Generating Ideas

Some people are concerned about not knowing the right answer. One of the coolest things about outside-in marketing is that we don't expect you to. It's actually your customers who know the right answer. Your only job is to generate enough ideas that one of them turns out to be better than what you do now.

Luckily, improving what you have isn't always that hard, especially if you took our advice to start with the content that showed up the worst on the metrics we listed earlier. I mean, don't you think you could come up with a few ideas to improve a page with a 90% bounce rate?

The other good thing about generating ideas, as opposed to knowing the answer, is that the metrics discussed above usually contain great clues about what kind of experiments to run. If your bounce rates are high, maybe your page doesn't reinforce the concept that brought the person to the page, so try a few (dozen) experiments on that. If your engagement rate shows that people are not clicking on your critical link to the next step in the buyer journey, try making your content more persuasive—with a few (hundred) experiments.

If it seems daunting to do a few hundred experiments, there are ways to make it easier. One is to improve the content templates in your content management system (CMS). You can test judicious changes such as site navigation or offer placement or other site-wide experiments on a few hundred pages at once rather than on your whole site. This is called multivariate testing.

The other way to run experiments is with user testing, which is the subject we take on next.

Testing Ideas Before You Launch Them

Sometimes you can skip immediately to the next step—launching your fix and testing it in public—but many kinds of changes would be embarrassing or hard to reverse if you got them wrong. (Try changing your entire site back to its former visual design when the new one misfires.) User testing is the answer to this dilemma. You can recruit testers to privately try out your new brilliant ideas and let you know if you need to go back to the drawing board. There are two common methods of user testing:

- *In person.* The traditional (and more expensive) means of user testing is to bring real users into your studios and ask them to try to complete the user tasks in your experiences.

- *Online.* Becoming more common (and way cheaper) is speaking with real users on the phone while you are letting them use screen-sharing technology to use your new experience.

In either case, you give the testers a task to do, but you generally do not offer them any more direction. You ask them to say everything they're trying to do and enumerate all their frustrations during the task. You simply write down everything they say and make a list of possible things to fix from their narrative. After you fix all those things (or at least the ones that prevented the users from completing the task), you will be in a better position to launch your new experience—or to take the new experience through a further round of user testing.

Let's walk through an example. Suppose you have identified through keyword research that your audience needs a particular experience that you don't currently have on your site; this is often referred to as a content gap. How do you begin? The best way is to build a few trial designs and perform user testing with live users to see which one of your prototypes has the best chance of initial success.

The biggest value of user testing is the confidence it gives you that you're starting in a place that has a chance of success. If you launch a fundamentally broken site, you might never get enough data to iteratively improve it. User testing allows you to avoid this problem because once you get a dozen or so users to test an experience, you will tend to find similar problems and issues that they're having, which tells you what to try next.

So by now you are probably very excited about user testing as the answer to all your problems. Well, not so fast. There are a couple of serious limitations to user testing that you need to know so that you are not surprised when your testing occasionally sends you in the wrong direction:

- *User testing results are directional, not proven.* Unfortunately, as wonderful as user testing can be, it is usually unaffordable to run at the scale needed to be quantitative—where you are sure that you have the statistically significant correct answer. This means that it is very possible for you to have recruited a group of testers who are unlike your general audience in some unknowable way. This means that most user testing is anecdotal, or qualitative, in nature. Observing what real users do in real situations helps you notice blind spots that you had when thinking through the new experience, so that you can modify them and test again. And this open-endedness is one of the strengths of user testing because it can uncover problems you wouldn't even have known to test for. Be ready to throw out the result of any one test when statistically significant evidence calls it into question.

- *Some real-life situations are hard to simulate in a user test.* What really works for users sometimes depends on seeing a larger context than you can control in a user test. Consider Emily's case: She enters a keyword phrase into Google, clicks one of the links in the search results, and lands on a page. The relationship between the page she came from and the page she landed on is the most critical facet of the experience. How can you test this? If you just present her with your website's page itself and asked her to complete some information task, you aren't testing the relevance of the page to her search. But the alternative doesn't work well either; if you allow her to start by entering a search keyword into Google, Emily—and many of your other testers—will click on pages other than yours, so you might need a boatload of testers to get the answer you want. And telling them which page to click after the search makes the test almost as artificial as the original test, where you started Emily on your page after the search. Sometimes it isn't easy to simulate reality in user testing.

So, even well-done user testing can't tell you everything you want to know. Luckily, we have one last step that can overcome these user testing limitations, but it depends on your launching the new user experience to try it. That's where we go next.

Proving Ideas after You Launch Them

Precisely because there are problems with your experiences that you can never find solely through user testing, it doesn't pay to spend too much time trying to make your new pages perfect. You will learn far more after you launch than you could ever learn before.

You just need to be patient. Unfortunately, especially when you launch a new page, it can take three months or more for your pages to get significant organic search traffic from Google. This is where paid search is an important component to any content marketing effort. You need traffic to your experiences, and you won't get it naturally right away. But you can pay for it by buying the words the page is about in Google. This helps you bridge the gap in traffic until the page starts showing up naturally. Once you get enough traffic, you can continue testing your page live on the site.

The testing you use in this case is called *A/B testing*, and it's a simple concept with powerful implications. A/B testing is the practice of building two experiences that are similar in every way except *one* and then randomly serving them to users in an equal distribution to see which one works better. When the test shows you the winning version, you use the winner as the new version. And you build a new version B with some other aspect of the page changed. Then you test again.

While at some point you might run out of ideas for how to make the page better, many companies test the same pages with new ideas for years, constantly tinkering with them to make them slightly better on a regular basis.

Let's look at an example. If you have a page with a high bounce rate, you should be testing different versions of the body copy. If you have the keywords written in bold type in the first line of the body copy (a best practice), perhaps there's a different sentence construction that is more easily scannable. Testing different sentences that mean the same thing is a good way to get started with A/B testing.

But don't restrict your A/B testing to mere sentence construction. You can test heading styles, white space, fonts, pull quotes, placement, number of words in the body (start with 100 or so), and any number of other variables that might seem small but often make a big difference to users like Emily, who are quickly scanning for relevance.

When you get below the magical 30% bounce rate threshold, you might want to shift to other big problems the page has—such as bullet treatments in the body, the placement of the calls to action, the types of assets you use and their placement, the use of infographics and other visual aids, and so on—or move onto other problem pages. You will never be done testing the page, as long as it continues to improve with each new test.

A/B testing is not hard to implement. Many tools do all the work of randomly showing the two different page versions and counting which one garners more clicks in the right place. All you have to do is provide the two versions for the experiment.

How many tests should you run before concluding that you have the right answer? A good rule of thumb is 1,000 unique visits, but your testing tool can tell you the right number depending on how different the results are for A and B. The farther apart the results, the fewer visits you need to tell which one is better.

On your top-of-funnel pages, you might get a sufficient number of visitors within a week of launching the test. So you could get into a weekly cadence where you are testing a new thing every week. That's ideal. But if you are testing experiences about long-tail keywords, the cadence could be every two weeks or every month. If you have a smaller site, that might take a lot longer, so we'll forgive you if you are ready to take your answer a bit faster so you can run more tests.

You can also speed the process by running *multivariate tests*, which test more than one version at a time. You can have any number of variations on a single facet of your page, or you can test single variations of multiple different things on a page. The more complicated the test, the longer it takes to run enough tests to determine the winners. Having a competent analyst to run the test and evaluate the results is important to successfully using multivariate tests. So keep it simple and be content to run the tests on a cadence appropriate to the number of visitors to your pages.

Successful content marketing is a long-term effort. You launch, test, and iterate. Over time, as others recognize your experiences as good sources of answers to the questions implied by the search keywords, you will get links to your pages. This will help your ranking. Also, as fewer people bounce off your page and engage with it, Google will use this as a sign that it is worthy of a higher ranking. Your experiences will grow in traffic, which will lead to more data from your A/B testing, which will lead to faster improvements, which will improve your content's ranking—and the virtuous cycle continues.

The quicker you get your new experiences to market, the quicker they will ascend the rankings and become top generators of business for your brands. But most businesses have events or launch content that is out of date before it has a chance to get into good ranking positions. For this short-shelf-life content, your only hope besides paid search is to get picked up by one of the news sites, such as Google News. The process of building, launching, and iterating on this content is the same as it is for evergreen content, though there are differences in the way you perform keyword research. The main difference is speed. For short shelf-life content, you have even less time to get it to market and get it recognized by the news search engines. Here the build, launch, and iterate process is greatly accelerated; there is no prelaunch user testing.

Whether you are launching evergreen or short shelf-life content, the main point is to get it out the door quickly, learn how to improve it through A/B or multivariate testing, and commit to making those improvements. Good sites need regular care and feeding. Even when you rank well and generate good engagement and conversion rates, you should be experimenting with designs to test new patterns. There's always room for improvement.

Propagating the Fixes

UX professionals realize how long it can take to truly fix a problem once it has been identified. It can take a long time to identify the problem, generate the ideas, conduct user testing of alternatives, and then launch and iterate more fixes based on A/B testing. So, how can we get more leverage out of that hard-won knowledge of what actually works for our customers?

Patterns.

UX teams know that user behavior isn't unique to every different experience in a website. Once we fix a problem in one part of our site, we can find similar problems in other parts of the site and try the same fix. These similar patterns of behavior can be addressed with similar *UX patterns*. UX teams should be learning from each other.

Perhaps a non-content example might make it clear. Most websites have numerous pages that challenge visitors for their security credentials, such as an ID and a password. This seemingly simple interaction is actually rather complex, and you can tell that by how many different UX patterns exist around the web to satisfy this common use case.

Several components of a login UX pattern make these interactions easy for customers:

- Use common names, such as an ID and a password. If you call your password a PIN, some people will have more trouble with the experience.
- Let people use their email address as their ID because it will help them remember it.
- Provide an easy way for people to register if this is their first time.

- Provide a "forgot your password" link right inside the login interaction.
- Provide a check box to remember the ID and password for the next time but warn users not to check this box when using a public computer.

Now, not all websites follow these guidelines—sometimes for good reason. You need higher security for your online back account than for a private message board. But even though not all of these experiences are the same, over the years, some patterns have emerged to make the experiences more similar—and thus easier for users. It's at least true that every website should have the login experience be the same across the site.

So, how does this concept of patterns apply to your content experiences?

You start by identifying the characteristics of when the pattern is used. If a UX pattern has a particularly successful engagement, conversion, or advocacy rate, document it. What about that page was improved over all the others in your company? Who is the target audience? What was the buy cycle state? What assets are on the page? What other metrics do you gather from the page? If you can pinpoint the one thing that made the difference, everyone should know about it so they can apply the lesson more broadly.

The other teams that create and optimize experiences can perhaps shortcut the iteration process by adopting the most successful patterns. Every time a page breaks a new company record for low bounce rates or high engagement, conversion, or advocacy rates, celebrate it by codifying it into a pattern. Successful patterns can sometimes be specific to an audience or buy cycle state. So don't overgeneralize. But if your company has stored a successful pattern for your audience and buy cycle state, give it a try in one of your A/B iterations.

Larger content marketing organizations build pattern libraries, where all the successful patterns are documented, along with all the relevant facts about them. These become excellent training tools because designers don't just learn what works and what doesn't. They learn why—in the context of the team that built these experiences.

Pattern libraries are a form of internal publishing. They serve as a series of standards documents that are continually updated and improved. Unlike style guides, pattern libraries don't focus on designers' opinions of what looks good or not. They focus on the data that shows what techniques work in real-life examples.

Pattern libraries also give practitioners the recognition of a job well done. We recommend building incentives into the publication of new patterns. Build a template that all UX designers should follow, to ensure that all the patterns have a common data model. Put them on an intranet or a file-sharing site. Host regular lunch-and-learn sessions where a designer demonstrates the use of a pattern as a case study. And reward pattern publication the way engineering firms reward patent publications: with real money.

A good UX pattern library is an extremely valuable resource for your company, for a few reasons:

- It helps new designers learn what works and why.
- It serves as a living standards document for your designers.
- It recognizes good designers by documenting their successes for all to see.

As important as UX design is to a company, it always seems like an uphill climb with executives. There are no shortcuts. It takes time, talent, and discipline. We find that there are three essential features of clients that religiously propagate their UX fixes throughout their enterprise:

- They hire a UX practice lead whose job is to build and maintain the pattern library.
- They make it part of every UX designer's work to document every iteration—and to build patterns if they are particularly successful.
- They hold regular rituals to celebrate particularly successful patterns.

If you do these three things in your organization, you have a chance to make UX a competitive advantage for your company.

Wrapping Up: It's All About the Data

In this chapter (and throughout this book), we have intentionally simplified the concept of content marketing UX. We focus on inbound-marketing UX, and we have further focused on that part of inbound that relates to search. If you've read the rest of the book, you will know that there are two good reasons for this:

- Inbound is the most affordable and most effective marketing approach for most companies.
- The customer research involved in inbound content marketing provides data that you can use for any other marketing you do.

It's this second point that perhaps needs more emphasis. The data you gather from keyword research can be applied to any form of marketing. Data about how your audience searches for information is simply the best and most reliable audience data you have. Once you use this data to understand your audience, you can apply it to any number of other marketing activities, including branding, advertising, social media marketing, custom publishing, and even product marketing. Accurate audience data is the air marketers breathe.

The basic use case of engaging with users like Emily on and in her terms is applicable to every channel and tactic. You can apply the same audience analysis from search to the other places where your audience engages. A good example is YouTube, which is the second-largest search engine in the world but doesn't give you query data. So you have to use the data Google gives you and apply it to the YouTube channel, adjusting for all the things you know about YouTube users.

As we wrap up this chapter and the book as a whole, remember that content marketing is not an end in itself. Simply producing more and more content will not be enough because your audience is not going to have any more time to consume it. Because you can't win the content marketing war on volume, you must use the data available to you to pinpoint what your best audience—the one most likely to buy from you—really wants.

Big data is useful data only when you use it. Content marketing is nothing but noise when sprayed indiscriminately. By combining what you know about your customers with what they want to know about how you solve their problems, you create a level of relevance and of trust unknown to any other form of marketing.

Good luck with your content marketing efforts!

JARED SPOOL, ON WHY MARKETING MUST GO BEYOND ADVERTISING

Jared Spool is the founding principal of User Interface Engineering, a company that explores and maps the world of user experience and design. You can find an amazing amount of UIE's content marketing at http://uie.com.

Marketing has seemingly always been about advertising. You've been outspoken about the need for "delightful content." Why is that approach better than advertising?

It's a mistake to think that marketing is about advertising. I think advertising was predominantly the way marketers thought for ages because it fit into a certain model and came with the prestige of a budget. But the truth is that marketing is about getting your customer ready for a sale. It's all the work that happens to make the customer identify their pain, realize your product or service is a solution to that pain, and understand how to buy your product or service from you.

Advertising is a very narrow channel, where you push a message out and hope it lands. There's no interactivity—it's purely broadcast. And it competes against every other advertisement, at a moment that's probably inconvenient or disruptive to the person you're trying to reach. (Nobody likes having a movie interrupted for an ad just when it gets to the good part—except the advertiser.)

Contrast that experience with the content on your site. Potential customers seek it out. They use it to explore the topic and increase their understanding. Customers come on their own schedule. It's not a disruption. Instead, it's a welcome resource that can create delight in your audience.

Dana Chisnell, an expert on user experience and usability, has a wonderful framework for the concept of delight: pleasure, flow, and meaning.

When we talk about content marketing, *pleasure* mostly comes in the form of helping the customer realize there's a solution to a pain they're dealing with, which is the first step to solving any problem. It brings hope. If your content can help them realize that hope, that can be pleasurable. Pleasure can also stem from the realization that your solution is easy for them to implement. Knowing you can solve their pain without much falderal is a wondrous, delightful moment for many folks.

Flow is the process of identifying the solution through actually solving the problem. Cutting out all the unnecessary and frustrating parts of the experience will be delightful for your customer. Your content marketing can demonstrate how simple the product or service is. (And, of course, finding the content needs to be simple, too.)

Finally, there's instilling a sense of *meaning*. Customers will be delighted if your product or service connects with them in a meaningful way, such as connecting with their sense of protecting the environment or helping people in need. Your content marketing can expose the meaning and, if you craft it well, truly resonate with the important needs of your customers.

Of course, advertising can do all this, too, but the larger canvas of good content marketing gives a lot of possibilities and flexibility to the marketer. And it happens at a time when the customer wants it, not when it's likely inconvenient.

Content marketing seems like the flavor of the month right now. If everyone is doing it, why will it be any more successful than advertising?

Content marketing has been around for decades. Recipes, technical specifications, hobbyist magazines, medical brochures, and white papers have been providing useful, interesting, and even delightful information to prospective customers since the invention of retail. Its success is tied to how well it interests the reader. Content that doesn't help the reader explore a topic they are truly interested in will fall flat.

Content marketers need to spend more time researching the informational needs of their prospects. They have to learn which topics and which content resonates with their prospects. And they need to constantly curate their library to keep it current and helpful.

You're an expert in user experience, but everything isn't about user experience, is it? Advertising works, even though people don't welcome it. Doesn't it have a place in marketing?

Yes, advertising has a place if it connects with the reader and communicates exactly what they want.

Once, while we were conducting a usability test on how people read content on the web, we saw a woman respond to an ad. She was reading an article about being 14 weeks pregnant because, well, she was 14 weeks pregnant. At the end of the article, there was an ad for a book that promised to tell her what every week of her pregnancy would be like. She wanted to buy it immediately because she loved the content on the page. Had the ad been at the top of the page or on the site's home page, she would've skipped right past it. But because it was at the bottom of a lengthy article that had exactly the information she wanted to know about her life, she saw the value in the product. What she experienced was a "seducible moment," the point when an ad can be most effective because the user has been seduced into wanting to make the purchase by the content.

So, yes, advertising has a place in marketing. The problem is our advertising platforms make it hard to create seducible moments. Most ads are purchased never knowing what content they'll be next to, and algorithmic ad placement doesn't do a good job. I recently saw an ad for Samsonite suitcases algorithmically placed next to a story about murder victims whose cut-up body parts were transported in (you guessed it) Samsonite suitcases. Seducible moments require bespoke ad buys; without that, advertising's effectiveness will always be limited. But content marketing almost always has bespoke placement. That's what makes it work. Content marketing combined with seducible moment ad placement can be a truly effective arrangement.

Everyone is talking about big data, but user experience has traditionally been about small-scale user testing. How does big data affect user experience work?

Big data lets us make connections. When the analysis is done right, we can see patterns we wouldn't see in small-scale user research. For example, Netflix's use of big data makes its recommendation engine seem downright magical. But big data can't tell us why the connection exists. We can't know *why* someone who likes one movie also will like another without asking.

Content marketing, if it's to be successful, needs to be written with a thorough understanding of the *why*. It's the why that brings out the delightful aspects of pleasure, flow, and meaning. We have to go back to traditional user research methods, both in the lab and in the field, to understand why the connections are there.

How does your user experience background change the way you approach content marketing?

Well, funny you ask. Our research company has been using content marketing as its primary customer reach vehicle for the 26 years we've been in business. We've dabbled with advertising and other forms of marketing, but nothing has even come close to producing the returns of our content marketing efforts.

Because user research is in our DNA, we've studied why this is for years. We've looked at our customers' motivations and the problems they're trying to solve. And that's allowed us to hone our content marketing to its current level of effectiveness. We're constantly experimenting with new types of content, from videos to podcasts, to articles and free events. We can see what works and what falls short. We've gotten very good at this.

Content marketing also gives us a lens for viewing our client projects. As we're working with our clients on improving their effectiveness, we can use the research techniques we've honed over the years to see what's working and what isn't. It's been very successful for us.

Index

event marketing, 11-13
spending on advertising, 8-10
telemarketing, 10-11
versus inside-out, 5-6
over-emphasizing advertising, 72
pay-per-click, 9
pull, 11
separating from public relations,
    73
spending, 8-10
telemarketing, 10-11
versus customer service, 2-3
advertisements
banner blindness, 7
mistake clicks, 9
retargeting, 7
spam, 7
welcome, 7
Advertising Age, 8
advocacy, low rates, 150-151
AdWords (Google), 55, 82
agencies, overreliance, 111
artificial intelligence, 40
**attribution modeling, audience
    feedback systems, 99-100**
**audience feedback systems, 83,
    97-98**
attribution modeling, 99-100
key performance indicators, 98
*Audience, Relevance, and Search:
    Targeting Web Audiences
    with Relevant Content,*
    12, 121

audience research systems, 82-84
search keyword research, 84-87
social media listening, 87-88
auditing content, 114-116

B

Back Azimuth Consulting, 78
bank, advertising, 1-2
banner blindness, 7
Berners-Lee, Tim, 90
big data, 16-17, 118
analyzing social media as,
    102-108
four Vs, 31
platforms, 118
Bing
keywords, 4
search referrals, 33
blatant sales (BS), 27
blogs, 129-130
**body copy, scannable content,
    123**
Boolean queries, 102
bottlenecks, user experience, 146
fixing, 151-154, 157
high bounce rates, 147
low advocacy rates, 150-151
low conversion rates, 149-150
low engagement rates, 147-149
propagating fixes, 157-159
**bottom-up content strategy,
    114-115**
bounce rate, 33, 147